# Letters to a Niece

# Letters to a Niece

*Friedrich von Hügel*

REGENT COLLEGE PUBLISHING
*Vancouver*

**Letters to a Niece**

Originally published in 1928 as *Baron Friedrich von Hügel's Letters to a Niece* by J. M. Dent & Sons Ltd., London & Toronto [Edited by Gwendolen Greene].

Reprinted 1998 by Regent College Publishing, an imprint of the Regent College Bookstore, 5800 University Boulevard, Vancouver, B.C. V6T 2E4 Canada <www.regentpublishing.com>

The views expressed in this work are those of the author and do not necessarily represent the official position of Regent College.

Printed on demand in the United States and the United Kingdom

National Library of Canada Cataloguing in Publication Data

Hügel, Friedrich, Freiherr von, 1852-1925
  Letters to a niece

  ISBN 1-55361-029-6 (Canada)
  ISBN 1-57383-103-4 (International)

  1. Hügel, Friedrich, Freiherr von, 1852-1925—Correspondence. 2. Spirituality—Catholic Church. I. Greene, Gwendolyn Maud Parry, 1878- II. Title.

BX4705.H77A4 2001   248   C2001-910660-2

*25 April 1918*

My very dear Gwen,

Your Aunt Mary showed me your plucky letter received by her yesterday morning. I was in church at Holy Communion this morning, and I then prayed and thought very specially of my very dear Niece — that every deep, rich growth, happiness and faithfulness may attend and fulfil her life and work and sufferings and various joys. Four points occurred to me — I will put them down here for you, since now, lying up, you may care to let them simmer in your heart, and to get them to bloom into action or habit. This, however in proportion, *pray* — as any of it really comes home to, really fits your own sight or search — such things ought always to feel, at first, as just a size or two too big for us — as what gently stimulates us to a further growth and expansion; but they should always be quietly ignored, if, and in so far as they come before our quiet look at them as conundrums simply imposed on us from without.

(1) I am, then, really grateful (given you are run down and require a rest) that you are, plainly, much worn and tired — for only so would you give up for a bit, and get looked after properly, and thoroughly rested back into full power, and it will be delightful if, without straining, you can now and then quietly browse through that charming Boissier or Horace and Virgil — and perhaps this or that other of the books on Roman things.

(2) ...

(3) I continue much struck, my very dear Gwen, with your (very rare) youthfulness and keen ardour of mind. Your continuous openness to the impressions (fresh as ever) brought you by all things beautiful and true and good. Do you *realise* how rare this gift is? That it *is* a gift, one of the most precious of the gifts — of God? That it is a

form and kind of deep faith—a true prayer? I ask all this that you may mix with these admirations, more and more, little exclamations of gratitude, of union with, of adoration of God, present in all this truth, beauty, and goodness. You could gradually develop this into spontaneous habit.

(4) For years I have loved and prayed this prayer, Dearie. If it makes sense to you, you too might begin your day with it. "Receive, O Lord, my entire liberty—my understanding, my memory, my will. From Thee I have received all things—to Thee do I return all things. Give me but Thy Grace and Thy Love. I ask not anything else of Thee."[1] ...

Loving old Uncle,
Freddy H.

*30 September 1918*

My very dear Gwen,
This is a letter all about your most dear father only, of course. But, being thus, you may not feel it inopportune—you may even like to have it for ruminamation since, though you must be longing to help, there cannot be much, at least of an external, practical kind, that you *can* do for him, just now.

Well, then, first I want to say how *deeply* I care, how *deeply* I mind. I have known your father for nearly half a century; during all that time I have been getting to know fresh people, and have been getting to know those I knew already far more widely and deeply, I believe. And yet I have never, before those years or during them, known a man so utterly generous, so essentially lovable, as your father. Of course I know well, besides, that he is a real

---

[1] St. Ignatius.

genius — a genius of a large, rare kind — a genius in music. But though I admire this, and I thank God for it — this, in itself, is nothing lovable. What I love so in him is his radiant lovingness — that rich spending, without thought of its being anything other than simply natural, utterly delightful, of a loving heart, upon whomsoever he may meet who at all appeals to it. And the appeal is felt to come, not from the apparent cleverness, or riches, or charm, but simply from the fellow-creature's need and cry for help and sympathy. What an untold *world* of kindness, of paternal help and warmth, he must have given away throughout all these years at the college.

It is, then, a deep, deep grief, Gwen, to have to fear, from your letter, that we are probably about to lose him, in and during this our little earthly life. Then, next, I want to confess to you a prick and a pang of conscience which has been with me concerning him ever since we travelled down to Wilton together for your Uncle Mingo's funeral. I suppose I was overwrought or something else odd and abnormal, but, anyhow, I told him in starting on the journey, that I did not want to converse — especially not about music. Alas, alas: how rude, how impertinent, how entirely contrary to my own self when reasonable at all! I have longed to find the opportunity to beg his kind pardon for this — but have never seemed to find it without making a fuss somehow. So, my dear child, you who have inherited so much of his glorious generosity — tell God for me, by your father's side, how deeply I love him, how vexed I continue with myself about that silly act of mine.

And lastly, my Niece, let me say one little word about a much deeper matter. Your father, Dear, like your also fine-charactered uncle, George — grew up, and lived to middle life, during a religiously sceptical time — they could hardly escape that all-pervading atmosphere — in any case they did not escape it. I love to feel that, even in those times, your father believed more than he thought he

did; and again that, since then, he has quite possibly silently come to considerably more belief, even in his own
consciousness concerning his convictions. I should dearly
like, if he is still sufficiently, for short whiles, himself, that
you should ask him quite simply to affirm his faith, his
love in God—or, better still, some little aspiration directly
to God Himself.

With entire resignation into His hands,
F. v. H.

*9 October 1918*

My very dear Gwen,

Oh, we are sad at his having gone—the generous, simple, loving soul—the genius with a heart of a boy and yet
with all a father's tenderness for quite a world of souls.
You evidently expected this ending—you—Gwen, did. But
your mother, poor thing, may have gone on hoping to the
end, in which case the shock of his going will, we fear, be
all the greater. How devotedly he loved on, from the first
and unceasingly to the end! There, too—so fine a man; for
such things are not mere accidents—they show a man's—
his—nobility of nature.

I trust and fancy that he did not suffer much, even at
the end. If so, that will have been a great relief to you all,
for him so extra-alive, so sensitive a constitution and nature. Much as I feel for you, very dear Niece—for you so
like him in many ways—and for Dolly, who also loved
him so much and who was so much loved by him: I yet
feel most sorry somehow—next, of course, to your mother
—for that world of his at the College of Music. The loss to
hundreds of men and women, young and now middleaged, who were there, or are still there—must be literally
irreplaceable—irreparable, because your father was not
simply a man who knew his business—nor even a man of

4

real or great talent; no, but because he was a man of deep genius, and who, as such, could divine when any scraps of genius were lurking in others, and irreparable, even more, because his combination of such genius with his, in any walk of life, most rare steadiness and volume of self-less interest and affection — of truly parental character — is doubtless specially rare amongst musicians. Certainly Beethoven was not like that, nor Wagner. ...

Forgive absence of mourning paper.

13 VICARAGE GATE, KENSINGTON, W. 8

*11 December 1918*

My very dear Gwen,

No letter you will ever write to me shall, please God, ever remain unanswered — shall remain without a reply as careful and complete as I can manage to make it. But you may have to wait a bit, my Niece. I never could write with ease — not on such subjects, where we should never write, speak, or think except with *voce di petto*, never with *voce di testa*. And now I am still weak, and empty of brain, hence a further delay.

Let me make *three or four points* of your letter; and try to explain these as well as I now can manage.

1. *The gradual preparation for, and God's revelations preceding, His fullest self-revelation in Christianity.*

I am very glad you apprehend and appreciate this great fact — a fact, however, which you will have to learn to apply, not only to *the succession of history*, but also to the *simultaneous present*. What I mean is that, not only was Judaism especially, yet also, in lesser and other degrees, Hellenism, Hinduism, etc., an historically previous preparation by God Himself for the fuller and fullest self-revelation; but this *holds still* of those imperfect, mixed forms and degrees of light, in so far as they still continue distinct in the world. The synagogue here in Bayswater is

5

still now, on 11 December 1918 a fragmentary but very real revelation of God and, however unconsciously, a very real pedagogue to Christ. The little mosque at Woking is still, for some souls, a yet more fragmentary but still real revelation of God and teacher of truths more completely taught by Christianity. All this, however, only in so far as the souls thus helped have no interior incitement to move on and up into a fuller, truer religion. And nothing of all this means that these various religions are equally true (or false), and that it does not matter to which you belong (provided only you are in good faith). No: in these deepest and most delicate of all matters, even a little more light, more power, more reality—even what "looks" a "little"— means, and is very, profoundly much. It all only means, that nowhere does God leave Himself without *some* witness, and without *some* capacity on the part of the soul *(always more or less costingly)* to respond to, and to execute this His witness. And, again, that everywhere the means and the process are from fidelity to the light already possessed (yet often difficult to see owing to the agitations and cowardice of the soul), to further light, which again, in its turn, demands a delicate, difficult fidelity and fresh sacrifices. Yet with each such fidelity and sacrifice, the peace, the power, the joy, the humble fruitfulness of the soul grow. Always it is a search for expansion and happiness, found in acts gently costly and increasingly exacting.

2. *Only the best attractive to you; and any, every church, very middling, hence dull, repulsive. Thus you do not go to country church services, etc.*

The touching, entrancing beauty of Christianity, my Niece, depends upon a subtle something which all this fastidiousness ignores. Its greatness, its special genius, consists, as much as in anything else, in that it is without this fastidiousness. A soul that is, I do not say tempted, but dominated, by such fastidiousness, is as yet only hovering round the precincts of Christianity, but it has not entered its sanctuary, where heroism is always homely, where the best always acts as a stimulus towards helping towards being (in a true sense) but one of the semi-articulate, bovine, childish, repulsively second-third-fourth-rate crowd. So it was with Jesus Himself; so it was with Francis, the Poverello; so it is with every soul that has fully realised the genius of the Christian paradox. When I told you of my choking emotion in reading, in St. John's Gospel, that scene of Jesus, the Light of the World (that He is this, is an historic fact), as the menial servant at the feet of those foolish little fishermen and tax-gatherers, what do you think moved me but just that huge, life-and-love-bringing paradox, here in its fullest activity? The heathen philosophies, one and all, failed to get beyond your fastidiousness; only Christianity got beyond it; only Christianity. But I mean a deeply, *costingly* realised, Christianity — got beyond it: Gwen will, some day, get beyond it. It is, really, a very hideous thing; the full, truly free, beauty of Christ alone completely liberates us from this miserable bondage.

"Well, perhaps yes," you will say, "but what am I, here and now, to do?" Do, as to church-going, *nothing but what you already do*. Only be very conscientious and regular in going to your Holy Communions, whether in country or town, and in going to church every Sunday when you are in town. But as to your thinking and speaking, pray, and ruminate, Niece, over what I have been saying; look out in your readings for what confirms it; grow shy of any defence of fastidiousness; pray to God gradually to cure you of it, if and when you come fairly to see it to be a poor, a very poor, thing. You rightly dislike Pater's "affectation." What I call "preciousness." Well, in face of the dread facts of human nature, and of the rich teaching of history, that church-fastidiousness is a sort of Paterism.

3. *What is the precise meaning of Thekla's insistence upon religion as primarily an is-ness, not an ought-ness?*

A good question. Well, you see, Niece, when the Renaissance and the Protestant Reformation, and later the French Revolution came, they, in part, only articulated, but also they, in part, each differently, yet all greatly, fed and excited a reaction which had permeated the educated average man of Western Europe ever since, say, A.D. 1300. It was a reaction away from the (by then too exclusive) occupation with the object—with *things*, taken as though apprehended by us without our minds, and especially with *supernatural things*, taken as so different in kind from our natural endowments, as to require a sheer imposing from without—a simple plastering on to the human soul and mind. These doctrines, against which there came the reaction, are *not* the doctrines really held by the Middle Ages at their best—say, from A.D. 1100 to A.D. 1300, but they were the doctrines of the later, moribund Middle Ages, and they were doctrines by which those Renaissance, Reformation and Revolution doctrinaires were really profoundly infected—as is always the case with men who do not patiently study the past (also the more recent past) and who, instead of discriminating, condemn what is before them *as it stands*—who do not untie knots, but who cut them. Again, Dear, do you note? Life taken cheaply—"cheaply," I mean, because practised and sought outside of, and not within, and by working through, its entanglements! Well, now, these three (and other) specifically "modern" movements have been very largely dominated by a most ruinous, excessive, or even exclusive insistence upon the *subject*—your own (or at least humanity's) apprehending powers, feelings, etc. *These subjective* powers get, here, more or less taken as alone certain, as always the first facts in the order of our life and consciousness. Thus, a baby will be taken first to feel, know himself—or rather, his own feeling and knowing, and then gradually to discover an outside world—his mother's breast, his nurse's hand, his cradle soft or hard, etc. — all this being really less certain (in itself, or at least for his mind) than is his true feeling, knowing himself. You entirely follow?

Well, then, even more as to God — the supersensible, the Infinite — He is pushed still farther back amongst the late-acquired, the more or less doubtful "ideas," "notions," "perhapses." — The regulative notions for our conduct, the useful, more or less, working answer to our real difficulties amongst our real facts. — An hypothesis, "it is useful to live *as though* there were a God"? Kant's celebrated "als ob"? Conduct here alone is quite certain; but then, too, conduct alone entirely matters. Religion is here always directly dependent upon, it is but the (really derivative, though seemingly superior) sanction of morality. How different is real life, and the spontaneous attitude of all unsophisticated religion! In real life (all good psychologists and all careful theorists of knowledge are coming to see it) there is from *the first* direct contact with, direct knowledge of realities other than ourselves. Light and air, plants, animals, fellow-humans, the mother, the nurse: these are known together with ourselves — we never know ourselves except with and through those realities, and with and through our knowledge of them. Indeed, it is them we know best first; we know ourselves, at all adequately, only last of all. This knowledge of other realities less than human or simply human is never a knowledge through and through — it never simply equals the reality known. But it is a real knowledge of these realities, as far as it goes; realities which reveal their natures in their various self-manifestations. I know Puck as truly as Puck knows me; my knowledge does not merely extend to appearances of him — appearances hiding, and probably travestying, his mysterious, simply unknowable essence.

We thus certainly know other realities besides our human reality (whether individual or even collective). And mark you, if this very real knowledge of realities not ourselves, always lags behind those realities as they are in themselves: *this knowledge, nevertheless, is (or can be) fuller than any complete and clear analysis of it can ever be.* Thus reality comes first; then knowledge of it; then science of this knowledge.

What about God? Well, we must first of all become clear to ourselves that, *as with every degree and kind of reality*, we always apprehend Him only in, and with, and on occasion of, yet also in contrast to, other realities. Again, that this apprehension and sense of God is (where not worked up and developed by the great historical, institutional religions) very vague and general, if taken as something statable in theoretical terms. (Here again, then, is the difference between knowledge and science!) Nevertheless, thus defined, the religious sense exercises a *prodigious* influence. It is the religious sense, even at this stage, where it seems no more (on strict analysis) than a deep, delicate, obstinate sense of otherness, of eternity, of prevenience, of more than merely human beauty, truth, and goodness, which really keeps our poor little human world a-going. No great artist, no great philosopher or scientist, no great ethical striver will ever fully, consciously, and deliberately admit that what he strives to paint, to sculpt, to compose, or to discover or to understand, or to live and to be, is just human so-and-so-ness, very possible without any further significance or truth about it whatsoever.

We have to be truthful, conscientious: why? Because these are the dispositions for putting us into fuller touch with realities of all sorts, especially with the reality of God. Dispositions are the means to acquiring reality— towards knowing, loving, willing realities greater than ourselves—in which energisings we grow in our own smaller reality.

When, then, Thekla says "religion has primarily to do with is-ness not ought-ness," she means that religion is essentially evidential; that it intimates, first of all, that a superhuman world, a superhuman reality *is*, exists. The first and central act of religion is *adoration*, sense of God. His otherness though nearness, His distinctness from all finite beings, though not separateness—aloofness—from them. If I cannot completely know even a daisy, still less can I ever completely know God. One of the councils of the Church launched the anathema against all who should declare that God is comprehensible. Yet God too, God in some real sense especially, we can most really know, since as does even the rose how much more He? Since He deigns to reveal Himself to us. He does so in a two-fold manner—vaguely, but most powerfully—in the various laws and exigencies of life, and of our knowledge of it; and clearly, concretely, in and by the historic manifestations in and through the great geniuses and revealers of religion—the prophets, and especially Jesus Christ. These latter manifestations get thoroughly learnt only in and through the various historical religious bodies. It is through men trained through and through in these schools of religion that all the more solid and sane insights and habits, even of the vague religion, get given most of the point and steadiness which, as a matter of fact, they possess.

4. There is not a line of all the above which has not to be learnt in careful detail, in lowly practice, in humble daily fight with self—in docility and docility on and on. We will gradually, ruminatingly, get the whole unrolled before us. The all-important point is, I think, at each step to feel how rich, how inexhaustible, how live it all really is! That is why I am trying to get such words as "Rome," "Athens," etc. to mean a great rich world to you.

Gradually I shall give you more directly religious books to ponder; yet, to the end, these should be made to penetrate and purify a whole mass of not directly religious material and life. God is the God of Nature as of Grace, He provides the meal and the yeast. Let us act in accordance with this, His own action.

Affec. Uncle,
F. v. H.

*Extract from letter dated 23 January 1919*

I am sorry but not a bit surprised that you have been
finding *Varro* a bit dull – even though he be presented by
Boissier, who assuredly is in no wise the cause of this
dullness. But I felt, Niece mine, that I must thus risk, now
and then, say once in ten times, to give you something
that will a bit bore you. No: I felt something more and
other than that. You see, Niece, one reason why there are,
as I think, so few at all large, strong minds and characters
about nowadays, even in spite of the war, etc., is that
education, training of all sorts, religion even, have been
and are so largely pursued systematically as so much be-
guilement, so much sheer kindergarten. The dullness, the
monotony, the hardness, the sheer trust as to worthwhile-
ness, the self-discipline, the asceticism: all this is to count
as old fogey-ness: and the result is? Well, wayward childishness. At eighteen I made up my mind to go into moral
and religious training. The great soul and mind who took
me in hand – a noble Dominican – warned me – You want
to grow in virtue, to serve God, to love Christ? Well, you
will grow in and attain to these things if you will make
them a slow and sure, an utterly real, a mountain step-
plod and ascent, willing to have to camp for weeks or
months in spiritual desolation, darkness and emptiness at
different stages in your march and growth. All demand
for constant light, for ever the best – the best to your own
feeling, all the attempt at eliminating or minimising the
cross and trial, is so much soft folly and puerile trifling.
And what Father Raymond Hecking taught me as to spirituality is, of course, also true in its way of all study worthy the name. But *L'Opposition* and the big and little Juve-

nal will, I think, not bore you at all—all the less as coming from what did.

*The Letters of the Younger Pliny.*

These are truly silver literature, and without the genius that stamps the work of his close friend Tacitus as world-literature of the first rank. Yet how charming they are! How much I hope you will browse on these utterly leisurely letters and learn much—very much, not only about the Roman character already so pathetically but half, but a tenth part, aware of the great light and life and love of Christianity—but about the human heart, the human soul—what I aim at after all as the end crown of your reading.

How wonderful in this way is his letter to Trajan about the Christians—how delightful all his relations with that emperor, one of my dearest figures! How impressive his account of the fall of Pompeii, and so on and on! You will read it all please, at least twice, with the Life, etc., as well. I deeply regret that I have not been able to find a translation of P.'s *Panegyric of Trajan*—that touching piece. I will continue to try for perhaps a French rendering.

Your very affec. old Uncle,

F. v. Hügel.

Health, stationary still.

13 VICARAGE GATE, KENSINGTON

*31 January 1919*

My dear Gwen,

Thank you much for your good letter. I sent you this morning your new pagan—Rome, packet—five volumes, all of which are presents, so there is nothing even to come back this time.

Please attend to the following points:

## Letters to a Niece

I. The Virgil is, you will see, simply the second, last volume of the prose translation, and which you already possess ....

Altogether I should love it, if you ended by reading again and again all the first eight books of the Æneid; certainly the culmination of Virgil's lovely genius; the Sixth Book in particular has a mild splendour unsurpassed in all human literature. On the other hand I would counsel you against ever reading the minor poems—all given in this second volume. They are all very slight affairs, certainly *not* by Virgil, and quite unworthy of him. We have such grand other things to get through, and so many of them—we will not waste our precious time over insignificant trifles.

2. As to the Tacitus, I should wish you to do him first amongst the books of the packet. And pray study *the minor* writings first. I want you to read, very slowly, ruminatingly, comparing part with part, etc., the *Dialogue of the Orators*—it will teach you lots as to the strength and the weakness of this "silver age" Roman education. Next, the *Agricola*—this, like the *Dialogue*, at least twice, looking up all the British places on the map, and watching not only for interesting political and military details, but also for touches of the character of Agricola and of Tacitus himself—both such fine examples of the best Romans, who passed through the Terror under Domitian, on to the "Indian summer" of Rome's imperial times under Trajan, Hadrian, Antoninus Pius, and Marcus Aurelius. At least, this is true of Tacitus and of him only up to and into the reign of Trajan—upon the whole of Rome's happiest time during the four centuries of the Empire. The *Germania* I always feel to be much less rich in content than its two predecessors, still it *is* interesting, especially again nowadays. Perhaps one careful reading will be enough for this.

Only after all three minor writings and (of course) the translator's Introduction to them, will you tackle Tacitus's

*Histories.* Please first carefully study the Introduction, and use throughout very capitally clear maps in the covers — the maps in one volume whilst studying the other volume. Thus you can have the maps open before you all the time. But please note, not to force yourself to get any very clear, very detailed conceptions as to the successive steps of the campaigns, etc.; concentrate, on the contrary, on T.'s superb portraits of characters, and his always noble, majestic ideals and indignation. Even the vilest facts will not hurt you, when thus lit up and all their grossness consumed by this glorious soul's magnificent ardour. You could carefully mark these passages, and could then read these very carefully three times. Note, too, very specially, the entire book concerning the Jewish War and Tacitus's pathetic misconception of the Jewish religion, and of Christianity. This book is certainly to be read twice. — I believe now, after all, the *Annals*, which were my former favourites, are less perfect than these *Histories*. How I wish you knew Latin, to be able to read Tacitus's magnificence in his own language! Yet some of his splendour will reach you even in the English.

I am gradually getting your next packet ready — it is planned as the last pagan Roman packet, and will be, I hope and think, most valuable as a part of your course — it will lift up the Christian authors in all sorts of ways. — But, before then, you will carefully read, when Varro is mastered, also that charming *L'Opposition sous les Césars* (Boissier) with those grand Juvenal-Johnson poems.

What a fresh, further surprise and blotting-out of old landmarks is this General Election! I must not pretend to be other than very glad and relieved that the Coalition has been strongly backed and settled in. But three things in increasing order distress me. I feel that we must somehow have Mr. Asquith in the House; the returns by majorities of 8000 and 2000 respectively of such unprincipled but most mischievous wind-bags as Bottomley and Billings

shows sadly clearly the weak side of all democratic excitement; and the sweeping victory of Sinn Fein, and with
actually that woman lunatic returned in Dublin, shows
still more clearly how little men are really dominated only,
or even chiefly, by reason; in very large numbers, not by
reason, but by passion—a very different thing!

My dear Gwen, I trust that even already you feel what
a support against such windy impulsions, against such
wild rootlessness, is the habitual living in a world steeped
in history, in knowledge of the human heart—your own,
first and foremost, and, above all, in a sense of the presence, the power, the prevenience of God, the healing Divine
Dwarfer of our poor little man-centred, indeed even self-
centred, schemes. God bless you, then, Niece, at and for
the New Year, very specially.

Loving Uncle,

Freddy.

Best wishes also to your Harry, and to Olivia, Richard,
and David.

13 VICARAGE GATE, KENSINGTON, W. 8

*10 March 1919*

My dearest Niece,

You asked me in your last letter to write again soon;
and hence I do so, as to two points in your reading, and in
your mental habits generally, which I am confident you
will find of great advantage. I have myself practised and
tested these habits now for some thirty years with very
great fruit.

1. Whenever you study a book which is yours, cultivate
the habit of pencil-marking it, in a small hand, with a
sharp-pointed pencil, as follows: (i.) Use the *inner* margins
of the pages for references as to words, phrases—form
generally; and the *outer* margins for references as to persons, places, doctrines, facts and things generally. You

slightly underline, with a short horizontal line, the word or words that strike you. If they strike you as to *form* you put, on the inner margin, at the corresponding height of the page, the number of the other page or pages on which (before or after this page) the same word or phrase occurs. If the passage strikes you as to its *content*, you put on the outer margin the numbers of the other pages on which these contents occur again. In fact, you form your book into a sort of Reference Bible. Thus, for instance, in your Pliny the Younger, any special garden arrangements, or special points of his Bithynian administration, or particulars as to the heathen cults or as to Christianity, would be thus marked and marginally annotated with the numbers of the pages on which further details as to these several things can be found. Note, please, that for translations one only marks and refers for things; and that only in originals (hence, with you, only in books originally written in English or French) will one have underlinings for *both* things and expressions. Hence, Caesar, Tacitus, Pliny, etc., would only have outer margin references. But Boissier, etc., would have references also on the inner margins, just as Shakespeare, etc., would have them.

Then, on the fly-leaves at the *beginning* of the books that belong to you, I would, in short words of headings, put down the points as to things that you specially love, or have most learnt from, in the book, with the numbers of the pages in which these several things are discussed; and on the fly-leaves at the end of the same book, I would similarly put down the things I have not liked, that I object to.

You would find that this twice double system of annotation makes the reading sink ever so much more lastingly into you, and that only thus can you readily find again all the things that have specially helped you.

2. Strive hard (especially now you will be coming to the directly Christian books) to attain one of two possible

frames of mind. It will be only if you can manage to make the right frame of mind into your second nature, that you will deserve to grow in insight, love and fruitfulness, my little Gwen.

(i.) You could try and force yourself to see, or to pretend to yourself that you see, principles or convictions advanced by men holy or revered. Do nothing of the kind: you would only lose your sincerity, you would but prepare for yourself a dangerous reaction, and you would not really thus come to see a single step farther than you already see.

(ii.) Or (and this is, I think, for all of us the more immediate fault) you could concentrate on your own, present, explicit not-seeing of a thing, so as to decide that it does not exist, or (at least) that it never can or will be seen as true by yourself. This is doubtless the chief reason why so few minds grow in their outlook after, say, eighteen or twenty-one: they are so busy, pompously affirming to themselves and others that they don't and can't see this or that—that this is not, and that can't be—as to harden down, for good and all, into their narrow, stuffy little world. They thus confuse two very distinct things— sincerity concerning the insight they have got, with striving to acquire further, deeper, truer insight. It is, of course, profoundly true that we get to see more and better by being very faithful and very operative with regard to the light we have. But, then, this fidelity and operativeness should be very humble, very certain that there exist oceans of reality—of things and laws beautiful, true, good and holy, beyond this our present insight and operation. I so love to watch cows as they browse at the borders, up against the hedges of fields. They move along, with their great tongues drawing in just only what they can assimilate; yes—but without stopping to snort defiantly against what does not thus suit them. It is as though those creatures had the good sense to realise that those plants which do not suit them—that these will be gladly used up by sheep, goats or horses; indeed, that some of these plants may suit them—the cows—themselves later on. So ought we to do: not sniff and snort at what we do not understand here and now; not proclaim, as though it were a fact interesting to anyone but ourselves, that we do not, here and now, understand this or that thing; but we should just merely, quite quietly, let such things stand over, as possibly very true, though to us they look very foolish—as indeed, possibly, things that we ourselves will come to penetrate as true and rich indeed. In a word, we can and should be sure of all that is positive and fruitful for us in our outlook; sure, also, that whatever really contradicts *that* is false. But as to possible further truths and facts, we will leave ourselves peacefully docile and open.

13 VICARAGE GATE, KENSINGTON, W. 8

*7 April 1919*

My most dear Gwen,

Your letter has set me thinking—re-thinking your mind and soul, and how best quietly to feed and help them. I wanted to write an answer on Saturday, and then to-day. But my last four or five nights have been, upon the whole, so bad that I dare not yet write directly about your very important and delicate points, since, when I am in such "en-compôte" condition, such letter-writing means further bad nights. I will write as soon as I can. This is only a scribble, lest my silence were to end in making you fear indifference or offendedness on my part—neither of which would be at all the case.

I wonder whether you realise a deep, great fact. That souls—all human souls—are deeply interconnected? That, I mean, we cannot only pray for each other, but *suffer* for each other? That these long, trying wakings, that I was able to offer them to God and to Christ for my Gwen-child—that He might ever strengthen, sweeten, steady her in her true simple, humble love and dependence upon Him. Nothing is more real than this interconnection—this gracious power put by God Himself into the very heart of our infirmities. And, my little Gwen, it is the Church (which, improperly understood, "dumbs" my little old, bewildered Child)—it is the Church which, at its best and deepest, is just that—that interdependence of all the broken and the meek, all the self-oblivion, all the reaching-out to God and souls which certainly "pins down" neither my child nor this her old groping father—which, if it "pins down" at all, does so, really only—even taken simply intellectually—as the skeleton "pins down" the flesh. What a hideous thing the skeleton, taken separately is, isn't it? Yet even Cleopatra, when in the splendour of her youth, she had such a very useful, very necessary, quite unavoidable skeleton inside her, had she not?

But this will be better explained another time. Meanwhile we will both breast the waves, whether sweet or bitter, looking not at them, but through them on and up to God, our Peace.

13 VICARAGE GATE, KENSINGTON W. 8

*5 May 1919*

My very dear Gwen,

Here I am writing to you, in your new temporary home, looking out of your window, I expect, upon how much of past history recorded in gloriously beautiful monuments, poems in stone! And I am doing as my first act (after an urgent business card), on this my birthday, this my scribble to you. I am, dear, dear, sixty-seven years old to-day! Thus, dear Child—you might almost be my granddaughter—do I strive to attain to the joy of Princess Colombe, in Browning's touching play. You remember how she, Colombe, had, up to her coming of age, always received countless sumptuous presents—and she had found only pleasure, and less and less pleasure, in such receiving. So then she settled she would receive no gifts at all on this, the first day on which she could order her own life in her own way; but she would herself give and give and give. She felt *that* would bring—not pleasure, but joy, but beatitude. And so it did—Colombe finishes her day radiantly happy. So, then, sit on a footstool here, by me, Daughter; and I will try and give you—not exterior things, but interior things—things that cost one a lot to get, a lot to keep. They are things, indeed, that also cost one a good deal to give—and I can clearly tell you why, my Gwen. Look you, Dear: there is simply *nothing* that one soul can transfer to another soul—even at these souls' best—with the particular connotations, the particular experiences of heart and heart, of blood and breeding, of sex and age, etc., yet it is these particularities which incarnate the convictions of any one soul for that one soul. Any one soul can be fully impressive for another soul only if that first soul comes out, to the second soul, with its convictions clothed and coloured by those its particularities. And yet the second soul, even if thus impressed—even if it thus wakes up to great spiritual facts and laws—this second soul will at once, quite spontaneously, most rightly, clothe and colour these its new convictions with its own special qualities and habits and experiences of thought, feeling, imagination, memory, volition; and so—most really—to try and help on the life of another soul means, Dear, a specially large double death to self on the part of the life-bringing soul. For it means death to self before and in the communication—the life-bringing soul must already, then, discriminate within itself between the essence of what it has to say and the accidents, the particularities, which clothe the utterance of this essence; and it must peacefully anticipate the acceptance *at most* of that essence, and not of these accidents. And then, after the communication, this

21

soul must be ready actually to back the other soul in the non-acceptance even of the essence of the message, if there is evidence that the other soul is not really helped, but is hindered, at least for the time being, by this essence now offered to it. And, as already said, at best, *only that essence* can and should be taken over by this other soul, and the light-bearing soul, even then, must at once be busy helping the less experienced soul to clothe the newly won essence in clothing from the wardrobe of this other soul.

My Gwen, you see, this now, as follows, is the point which, with the sendings of books which I begin today, I hope you may end by seeing clearly, steadily, in your quite individual manner and degree. You see, *I* see, how deep, and dear, how precious, is your faith in God and in Christ. I thank God for them, and if to the end you cannot acquire, without really distracting or weakening that faith, a strong and serene insight and instinct concerning the great occasions and means by which those great faiths have been, and are still conveyed to, and articulated and steadied amongst mankind—why, then, to the end, I must, and will, actually defend you against the sheer distraction of such instincts and insights not actually possible to you. But it is plain that you would be a much richer, wiser, more developed and more grateful soul if you could and did permanently develop the insights and instincts that I mean. And certainly the things I am thinking of—their perception—constitutes just the difference between a fully awake, a fully educated mind, and a mind that is awake only as to results, not as to the processes; as to what it holds, and not as to who it is to whom it owes that it has anything large and definite to hold at all.

You see, my Gwen, how vulgar, lumpy, material, appear great lumps of camphor in a drawer; and how ethereal seems the camphor smell all about in the drawer. How delicious, too, is the sense of bounding health, as one races along some down on a balmy spring morning; and how utterly vulgar, rather improper indeed, is the solid breakfast, are the processes of digestion that went before! Yet the camphor lumps, and the porridge, and its digestion, they had their share, had they not? in the ethereal camphor scent, in the bounding along upon that sunlit down? And a person who would both enjoy camphor scent and disdain camphor lumps; a person who would revel in that liberal open air and contemn porridge and digestion: such a person would be ungrateful, would she not? — would have an unreal, a superfine refinement? The institutional, the Church is, in religion, especially in Christianity, the camphor lump, the porridge, etc.; and the "detached" believers would have no camphor scent, no open air, bounding liberty, had there not been, from ancient times, those concrete, "heavy," "clumsy," "oppressive" things — lumps, porridge, Church.

There is, most certainly, a further difficulty in this question. The Church, especially *the* Church in the most definite sense, the Roman Catholic Church, has at its worst done various kinds of harm, introduced complications and oppressions which, but for it, would not have been in the world. I know this in a detail far beyond, my Gwen, what you will ever know. But, my Dearie, let us keep our heads; and let us ask ourselves, not whether "Church" of any kind does not open the door to certain abuses special to itself, but, primarily, only whether *as a matter of fact* it has not been through the Church or Churches that Christianity has been taught or practised; that Paganism has been vanquished; that Gnosticism and Pantheism have not carried all before them, long ago: whether indeed it is not owing to the Church and Churches — to the organised, social, historical, institutional fact and tradition, that the most independent-seeming, the most directly inspired souls, do not draw a large part of the purest of their conceptions. Thus George Fox, the founder of the Quakers, taught that souls are each and all directly taught by God, and have no need whatever of Churches, institutions, etc.—all these latter things are so much obstruction and incubus. That he himself, at the end of two years of utter aloofness from all men, was taught directly from heaven (without any kind of previous initiation by any human being) that Jesus is the Way, the Truth and the Life; that God is Love; that to live is Christ and to die is gain, etc., naïvely admits that, during all that time, he had his *Bible* with him, reading, reading it, all those twenty-four months. And how that, after those entirely individual, entirely direct, utterly new revelations, he *did* find teachings in St. John's Gospel and Epistles, yes, not unlike his direct revelations; but these revelations were *in no way* suggested by those Bible passages, for these, Fox's revelations, were real, were revelations from the living God to his, Fox's, living soul—and how can something living be suggested by something dead? How can the Spirit be tied to the letter? How can anything but God Himself, and my own soul itself—these two working and responding directly in and to each other—how can or could they be otherwise than stopped or stifled by anything not themselves—by any person or thing other than just themselves in this their unique intercourse?

Now all this does not prevent Fox from having been a very spiritual man, and his good faith is transparent. Yet equally clear is the utter rottenness of his psychology and the childish simplicity of his conception as to the methods actually employed by God. For those beautiful thoughts, those great facts as to God and as to Christ, were they less beautiful, less great because they had been perceived and expressed already fifteen hundred and more years before Fox? And were they less Fox's own, was he less free in uttering them, because they had been awakened in himself so utterly freshly, by those lovers, thinkers and writers of the past? Nor would it be adequate to reply: "Ah, well, at

24

least the individual Fox was awakened by, or on occasion of, another individual, such two individuals do not make a Church, still less does that one individual (the Johannine writer) constitute a Church." Such a reply would be poor indeed. For the Fourth Gospel is already a *Church Document*—it already simply articulates the faith and love of the Christian community some sixty years after Our Lord's death. And even the whole New Testament, or also the oldest parts, even the unique life and love of Our Lord themselves; even these again presuppose a Church, a community, a tradition, etc., in which Jesus was brought up, and which He learnt from and obeyed till He transcended it, transforming and fulfilling all that was good in it.

You may ask, my Gwen Niece, what precisely I am driving at? Do I want to make you a Roman Catholic? Why, of course, no, Dear, I am busy, not with trying to get you to turn actively "churchy" even. I am hoping only to get you gradually to see the huge, unique, irreplaceable good that you, as we all, owe to the Church. Even if (which I hope may never happen) you came to find it somehow impossible to keep up as much of Church practice (Holy Communion, etc.) as, thank God, you practise now: even then you would (if I succeed) feel a deep, deep gratitude to the Church—something like to, though considerably more than, you will come to feel towards ancient Rome and ancient Greece. Want of such insight and such gratitude towards any of these forces constitutes always, I am sure, a very real limit and weakness.

Farther back, I said that the main point to consider was, not the harm done by churchmen at their worst, but the special function and work of the Church at its best. You see, Gwen, this is but the same principle which comes continually into everything. Take *marriage*. What a unique means of training the soul, how magnificent is its ideal! Yes, but nothing is, of course, easier than to collect volumes full of instances of infidelity, tyranny, non-suited-ness, etc. A good lawyer-philanthropist friend of mine has enthusiastically put forward the example of certain American states which allow sixteen valid reasons for divorce.

Take *parenthood*: what a unique relation, what an irreplaceable means for the mind's and soul's growth. Yes, but the volumes full of misguided parental affection or folly or tyranny! So with the *State*, so with *Art*, so with *Science*, so with all that the hands of men touch at all—hands which so readily soil even what they most need, what is most sacred. But notice how Church, State, Family, Children, the Marriage Tie, these, and other right and good things, not only possess each its Ideal, unattained outside of and above it. No, no: they each possess within them more or less of that Ideal *become real*—they each and all live on at all because, at bottom, they are necessary, they are good, they come from God and lead to Him, and really in part effect what they were made for.

Now the four sendings of books, beginning with this one, will specially invite you to note the action of *the Church within the Roman Empire*. The present five volumes deal with *the Church's Triumph over Paganism*; the next batch will deal with *the Church's Triumph over Gnosticism*; and the last two batches will deal with the hermits, monks, and three or four of the largest minds amongst the Roman Empire Christians.

As to this batch, read, my Dear, as follows:

1. Wiseman's *Fabiola* (a gift). The parts descriptive of the Catacombs, Christian rites, etc., two or three times.

2. Allard's *Persecutions*, vol. i. The Acts themselves two or three times—the rest at least once.

3. Prudentius's *Cathemerinon*. I hope you will care to learn some of these hymns, so full still of the sense of all that Christianity had cost, and of how it was worth, oh, all *that* and much more besides!

*Baron Friedrich von Hügel*

And 4. Then Allard's *Persecutions*, vols. iv. and v. Allard will thus give you the beginning and the end of those centuries of persecution. I hope that the Prudentius break will prevent the Allard affecting you too much. You will sincerely tell me how it all goes.

I trust the Salisbury time will refresh and rest you, my Gwen Niece. Kind regards to Miss Edith Olivier, with whom I used to have good walks and talks in Wilton.

13 VICARAGE GATE, KENSINGTON

*6 May 1919*

Your post card just came, crossing a long letter and five books from me. I did not, in fact, explain in that letter the following: (1) The *Fabiola* book, though not actually great, is yet a thoroughly useful thing: it was written after many years' frequentation of the Catacombs, and much living in that early Christian world. And it is thoroughly readable—witness its translation into thirteen different languages. The Allard volumes are very sincere, reliable, first-hand work—better far than anything in English on the same subject. I do hope you will love Saints Felicitas and Perpetua—the sweet virility, the tender strength of them! The Prudentius is, I believe, well done. Prudentius is no genius like Lucretius or like Virgil, but Prudentius is possessed by an insight and by facts far, far deeper than Lucretius or Virgil ever grasped. And he breathes a rich, utterly unsentimental peace—because a peace after and in struggle, suffering, self-oblivion.

Getting out all fine days now.

Uncle H.

13 VICARAGE GATE, KENSINGTON

*8 May 1919*

My dear Gwen,

Many thanks for your little letter acknowledging the *Persecutions*—books—and my long outpourings as to Church.

My post card will have reached you later. I shall love in due course to hear all your impressions as pat and fat as you can make them. But this has nothing to do with all that. It simply wants to tell you that we leave this for kind Cousin Evelyn de Vescis, Clonboy, Englefield Green—on Thursday—and stay there possibly till September—and that we much hope you will be able to manage a full week with us there. In this I would read aloud to you, say, Browning's great *Ring and the Book*—or some other amongst those I want you to know, that you may happen not to have read so far. And we could have thorough, easy, all-round talks in that pretty Surrey garden.

P.S. Delighted you like Tertullian! Mind you read the "Apology" very carefully—also the "Testimony of the Christian Soul." But indeed all the treatises translated in that "Library of the Fathers" volume are studded with jems of thought, faith, love of the purest water.

13 VICARAGE GATE, KENSINGTON

*14 May 1919*

This, my dear Gwen, is only to say two little immediately practical things ....

(2) I am delighted at your going to listen for three days to Edward Talbot, whom indeed I know, and whom I like and trust very truly. He will be able to put before you a large, fine amount of that really unlimited experience, wisdom, practicality, gained and transmitted by the Christian Church. You will gain much if you go simply without a

touch of cautiousness — leaving quietly what does not help — using gratefully whatever may, upon prayerful reflection, really help.

Pray for me there and always, Niece mine.

H.

*12 June 1919*

My most dear Niece,

I have been revolving your letter — its points — in my old head and heart, and the following is the upshot. I begin with the books and end with direct life.

1. I am glad you have read *Paradise Lost*, and still more glad that you do not like it. Rabindranath Tagore, at Vicarage Gate, told me that all his life he had wondered why Englishmen considered Milton a poet at all; for that to be a poet is not, primarily, to have a keen sense for poetical forms, but to be penetrated by a love of all things good in Nature, as vehicles and presentations of the spiritual realities — that an innocent sensuousness is a *sine qua non* for all real poetry. But that Milton is, in his heart of hearts, doubly cold, doubly hostile to Nature — good Nature. That he is incurably a Puritan; and then has also taken over the cold side of the Renaissance. I think myself that you are more just than Tagore, and that those exquisite early and short pieces *are* true poetry, are innocently sensuous. I feel the same with *Lycidas* and *Comus*. But Tagore is right as to the poet in *Paradise Lost* — all but grand bits, such as the invocation of light, his blindness, the description of Eve in Paradise, etc. The fact is that Puritanism is neither natural (in the good sense) nor (really) Christian.

2. As to Shakespeare, he is, indeed, an utter marvel of richness. But in Shakespeare I always end by feeling a limit in a way the very contrary to Milton's limit — yet a grave limit still. Shakespeare is a true child of the Renais-

sance also in the *Renaissance's limitation.* He has not got
that sense—not merely of life's mystery, etc.—but of the
supernatural, of the other Life, of God, our Thirst and our
Home—he has not got what Browning—on these points—
has so magnificently. No dying figure in Shakespeare
looks *forward*; they all look *backward*; none thirst for the
otherness of God, they all enjoy, or suffer in, and with,
and for, the visible, or at least the immanent, alone. When
the soul is fully awake, this is not enough; it only arouses,
or expresses, man's middle depths, not his deepest
depths. It is not anti-Christian; it is even Christian—more
Christian, really, than Milton—as far as it gets; but it does
not reach the ultimate depths, it never utters the full
Christian paradox and poignancy.

3. As to the Martyrs, I well understand, Dear, that you
have had enough of them, at least for the present, yet I do
not regret sending you the Allard. I am profoundly convinced that we can never be impressed too much by the
*reality,* the transforming, triumphing *power* of religion—by
the immense factualness. And for the purpose, I know
nothing more massively impressive than those first three
centuries of persecution. But it is literature, doubtless,
more for a mature or elderly man, rather than for a young
woman. And you will be able to feed the *astringent* emotions (alongside of the sweet) in other ways. This, of
course, means that I hold these astringent emotions and
moods—this apparent hardness, this combat and concentration, this asceticism, to be, in the right place and proportion, an absolutely essential constituent of the Christian outlook. Of course, a child can and ought to have
only a very little, and a peculiar kind of it; a woman ought
to find and to foster a form and amount of it, different
from a man's needs. But where this element is not, there is
not authentic Christianity, but some sentimental humani-
tarianism, or some other weakening inadequacy. By all

means return now, to Vicarage Gate, the three Allard volumes.

4. I had got you your next parcel made up of books about Gnosticism and the Church's immortal victory—in the first two centuries—over that many-headed monster, so live again amongst us. I had got passages from the chief Gnostics for you in English; such Pagan *Magic* writers and attempters of a Gnostic-Magic substitute for Christianity as Apuleius and Philostratus *(Life of Apollonius of Tyana)*. And I had finished up with Ibsen's grand, little-known play picturing these last attempts—for those times—of Paganism in competition with Christianity. I had all this ready, again, to bring home the reality, the irreplaceableness, of Christianity; and to protect you, through the self-expansion we can attain by history, from the Esoteric Buddhists, the Spiritualists, etc. The Gnostics of our day, very small descendants of those ancient Gnostics, who, bigger though they were, could not prevail in the fierce testing of human life.

But I see you are hungering now, not for the knowledge of things to avoid, but for the further revelation of realities to love. And so I am putting this Gnostic packet away for the present. I will take it when we have done the Pagan and Christian Greek things; as a matter of fact, Gnosticism *was* primarily Greek, though it broke out as a spiritual epidemic, at its worst, in the late Roman Empire.

5. I send you instead, by Hillie for two nights at Vicarage Gate, the following four books—two gifts and two loans. Pray read them in the following order, and with the precautions and considerations I shall now propose.

(i.) The *Octavius* of Minucius Felix.

I think this is the finest Latin Christian pre-Constantinian document, *as so much literature*. It is touching and helpful also spiritually; but as to depth and power, there exist greater things in that range of documents, e.g. Tertullian. But then Tertullian is disfigured with every kind of vehemence, want of proportion, bad taste in details, sometimes even in great things. Whereas Minucius Felix is so beautiful throughout his form, that Boissier loves him for it. You remember Boissier's fine analysis of the *Octavius*? Read, then, this short piece, very carefully, ruminatingly, at least twice—the Introduction first of all, and at the end of the second reading.

(ii.) Turmel's *Tertullian*.

Turmel is an excellent initiator into Tertullian, and will give you, I think, a vivid sense of what a genius, what a dazzling variety, what a harshness and impossibleness that poor great mind, that vehement, burning and largely burnt up soul, was in real life, and is still in his very difficult, largely repulsive, but astonishingly *live* books. You will never forget, will you, Gwen, that Rome—that official Christianity—deliberately and continually refused to accept Tertullian's tone, or to endorse his Rigorism? He ranks as the greatest of the *Montanist* heretics. And most undoubtedly Rome was right in all this, and Tertullian was wrong. Yet it remains simultaneously true, that Tertullian's is the first mind and personality of the first rank, classable as Christian, indeed heroically Christian in intention, that God gave or permitted to mankind, after the long break since St. Paul. Our Lord, the Unmatched, the Inexhaustible—God with us, surrounded by little, little men. And then, promptly, one great follower, St. Paul. And then a long break, followed by a second great follower, Tertullian. And then a shorter break, and a third great, indeed a still greater, a far mellower, a far more fully Christianised Christian man, St. Augustine. You will at first hate Tertullian as much as the Milton of *Paradise Lost* perhaps. Tertullian, a lawyer by training, and a hard, fierce, African Roman by temperament—with all the tendency to excessive reaction and vigilant rigorism of most converts—especially of converts from the moral corruptions of that late Paganism, can seem—can be—along cer-

tain of his most numerous sides—as legalistic, as merce-
nary, as cold, etc., as Milton. Yet all this, surrounded by
so much more, and the whole as part of a personality full
of vehement *exuberance*—a personality which, though it
can shout unjust reproaches and apparent arrogances, is,
at bottom, pathetic in the sense of its own unloveliness—
so in his little treatise on *Patience*, a virtue, he confesses at
starting, which he, the vehement, the turbulent, never possessed. Please note, too, that Tertullian stands quite
unique in the way he has always been treated by the official Church. A man once declared a heretic, and his writings were shunned by all but a few orthodox scholars, and
his writings would never be used with admiration and for
acceptance. But Tertullian was taken by St. Cyprian as
his, the bishop's, daily spiritual reading; and, indeed, St.
Cyprian's own writings are full of reminiscences of those
of Tertullian. And even in our recent times—upon the
whole more strict amongst the orthodox than were those
earlier centuries—this same privileged treatment remains:
there exists, e.g., a three-volume *Selections from Tertullian*,
made ready for sermons throughout the Sundays and
holidays of the year: this by a French priest in the forties or
fifties, with full episcopal approbation. Why has Tertullian always enjoyed this quite exceptional treatment? It is,
I think, not so much because he was the first to coin a
whole string of striking technical terms, which were taken
over permanently by Christian, especially by Latin Christian theology, but because Tertullian's errors were mostly
excesses in opposition to the natural, the first impulses of
the average man or woman—thus these errors were, upon
the whole, harmless.

(iii.) Tertullian, English translations of some of his chief
writings, in the "Library of the Fathers," vol. i.

Although Turmel will already have given you well-
chosen, well-translated extracts from Tertullian, I should
like you to read, in this (very fine) English translation, the

great "Apologeticus" — so amazingly rich in vivid pictures
and in vehement emotions—and the beautiful, deep
"Testimony of the Christian Soul." I have deliberately
withheld from the packet a good English translation of the
"Testimony of the Martyrs" and (again) of his "Testimony
of the Christian Soul"—a little volume like the Minucius
Felix. I have so acted because I do not want to give you a
second Tertullian volume, unless and until I find that you
are more helped than repelled by the fierce African. Of one
thing I am sure: no one can get much out of Tertullian
unless the person, man or woman, be thoroughly self-
disciplined, self-trained in the fruitful art and virtue of
gathering roses amidst thorns, and of discerning jewel
eyes in a toad's head. I want my niece to end by becoming
such a discriminator; how weary I am of the *lumpers*, the
whole-hoggers! I will not press you, over the Tertullians,
as to the amount of reading of him. You may find even a
single reading of the Turmel volume, as of the "Apologeticus" and "Christian Soul" in the "Library of the Fathers" volume, more than you can stand. Or again you
may discover refreshing oases in that scorching desert,
and may be drawn on by a genius, as certainly a genius as
he requires bucketsful of expansion and of sweetness to
render useful and palatable even thimblesful of his rigid-
ity and bitterness. If you are thus fascinated, a double
reading of Turmel, and a double reading of the English
volume (at least of the two pieces proposed) would certainly not be too much.

(iv.) Palladius, *Lansiac History of the Early Monks.*

Gwen will think that her old Uncle has never done with
astringency! My Gwen: just only you get inside any one of
the deeper and deepest *men* souls, when fully awakened
by grace, and you will perhaps marvel at, you will certainly have to note, the large presence—in very various
forms, no doubt—of such astringency, so if it be only to
understand the history of *men's* souls, a considerable ac-

quaintance with such pickles and prickles, such salt and such mustard, is necessary. Besides, as to this Palladius book in particular, it admirably balances and completes your outlook upon dying Paganism and upspringing Christianity in the decadent Roman Empire. Also, you can hardly understand well the St. Jerome and the St. Augustine volumes, of the packet to follow, unless you know something about St. Anthony and his companions. I shall be interested to hear whether my little old Gwen manages to discern, in these often strange scenes, a necessary, abiding element (capable of all sorts of forms and of degrees) of Christianity itself. There is still a strange (at bottom childish) intolerance abroad as to the ascetical element; but men—the deeper ones—are again coming to see what they had far better never ceased to see—so Professor William James, so too Professor Ernst Troeltsch—both men of the largest outlook. If you like Palladius, read him twice; if you don't, put him by till you can appreciate him, Dear.

6. As to worldliness—well, yes, my Gwen, it is a thoroughly vulgar thing, especially when we remember the *regal* call of our souls. You know and you feel this; and you have only to try and to do better and better—to fail, in this respect, less and less often, less and less fully. There is, however, one consolation about this—worldliness is a less dangerous foe of the spiritual life than is brooding and self-occupation of the wrong, weakening sort. Nothing ousts the sense of God's presence so thoroughly as the soul's dialogues with itself—when these are grumblings, grievances, etc. But, of course, the ideal is to do without either worldliness or brooding. I say all this, whilst confident that you do not class a right amount of (and kind of) sociability and of pleasure in it, as worldliness. Of course such social activity and pleasure is right, and indeed a duty and a help to God.

7. I love to think of the happy times you have had in Westminster Cathedral and now in Salisbury Cathedral. I take it that God in His goodness has granted you the simple Prayer of Quiet—or, at least, that you get given touches, short dawns, of it, now and then. You know, dear, how much and often I insist with you on the visible, the historical, the social, the institutional. But this is done without even the temptation to doubt, or to treat lightly, moments of formless prayer. Such formless prayer, where genuine, is, on the contrary, a deep grace, a darling force and still joy for the soul. May you have, and keep, and grow in this grace! What are the tests, the conditions of this genuineness? They are two. Such prayer may never become the soul's only form of prayer; formal, vocal or mental prayer—the reciting of e.g. the Our Father, the Glory be to the Father, Acts of Faith, Hope, Love, Contrition (as in the prayer-books or made up by oneself)—prayers, all these, we can give an account of when we have done them: such prayers must never completely cease. And such formless prayer is the right sort if, in coming away from it, you find yourself humbler, sweeter, more patient, more ready to suffer, more loving (in effect even more than in affection) towards God and man; given the first (precaution) and this second (result) you cannot well have too much of this prayer. And I think God will lead you much along this path; and that you will get beyond the worldliness, and other faults, especially through it. For you will get to love it so; and it will grow or will intermit, in proportion as you are faithful in turning away from self. A homely heroism will feed this prayer of speechless love; and the speechless love will feed the homely heroism.

*Baron Friedrich von Hügel*

CLONBOY, ENGLEFIELD GREEN, SURREY

*3 July 1919*

My darling Gwen-Child,
Your two letters about the Canterbury Retreat were,
and are, a deep satisfaction and joy to get and to ponder
over; only our having three friends staying here, and my
nights having, anyhow, become bad from doing too much,
have kept me from writing at once. And even now I feel I
had better not embark on your big learned questions—
gnosticism and earthly progress, but I had better merely
give you some impressions and suggestions directly connected with the effects of that Retreat or with the details
of your coming here.

1. As to your visit here ....

2. As to *Ring and the Book*, I had not realised the very
happy fact that you knew it well already—you shall have
the book from me here, but I think we had better not do
more with it than just compare our choice of finest pieces.
For I want to use these few precious hours to start you in
St. Augustine in his *Confessions*. I have two precisely similar copies ready for this meeting; so you can follow in *your*
copy what I shall read out to you from *mine*. I think this
may well be the best way for you to begin St. Augustine,
to do so with one who has tried to live the *Confessions* at
their deepest these last fifty years—so stop till Thursday,
Dear!

3. I so well understand both your deep helpedness by
Edward Talbot and by the services; and, again, the dullness of the lectures on St. Francis of Assisi (entrancing
subject though this be!), and your longing to get away
from all that ladies' chatter. As to this latter, it almost
looks as if you had no rule of silence (entire, or with but a
break of an hour a day, say). Yet this is a point so obvious
and so important, that I expect you did have silence, but
only that the ladies, even so, managed, over questions or

37

the like, to get in much dissipating chatter. Certain it is
that at no time is overmuch talking compatible with spiritual growth; to learn interior silence, the not talking to
self—our little notions petted as our own, etc.—is fundamental in the attaining of the spiritual life.

4. I especially understand the genuine, even great pain
that growth caused you, Gwen. A very good sign. Truly,
you understand, and will cultivate the knowledge, of two
facts or laws, Dear, won't you? The first is that our ideal
must be, in and for the long run—a genial, gentle, leisurely
expansion—no shaking of the nerves, no strain, no semi-
physical vehemence, no impatient concentration—suffering and (involuntary) strain may come to us; but all this
will, where good, be upborne and expanded into peace
and humble power, if we keep little in our own eyes, gently watchful, and united to God in love. The second fact or
law is that nothing we may feel, think, will, imagine, however spiritual, however *real* spiritually, but has, in this our
earthly lot, to be paid for in the body. True, the joy of it
will even do our body good: still a certain subtle, uninten-
tional strain has been introduced into our nervous system.
The same, in its degree and way, would be true, if we took
systematically to music or to mathematics. There is no
necessary harm in this, and no means of fully avoiding it.
Yet, it is important we should be aware of the fact. For
such awareness will help to give us a certain sobriety and
moderation in all this our emotional life—a sobriety and
moderation which will, if wisely managed, greatly add to
and aid that fundamental Christian virtue—creatureli-
ness.

5. And lastly—*consolation*, Dear, is sooner or later followed by *Desolation*; and the latter is, when and where
God sends it, and we have not ourselves brought it on
ourselves by laxness and dissipation, as true a way to
God, and usually a safer one, than consolation. Day and
night, sunshine and storm, union and aloneness—*both* are

necessary, sooner or later, Sweet. But, of course, it is for God, for Him alone, to leave and to apportion these vicissitudes to each soul. And certain it is that it is of much help to have some older, more experienced soul handy also, who can and will, if and when we get into Desolation, cheer us on, by the reminder of the former consolation, and still more by the great fact that only through such vicissitudes — through fidelity in them — can we grow strong and deep in God and for Him.

Loving old,
Uncle.

CLONBOY, ENGLEFIELD GREEN

*5 July 1919*

My darling Niece,

As to Traherne, Vaughan, Crashaw (I add Herbert and Donne), I think they all contain much spiritual food — one could easily make one's spiritual reading for several years of them, if their form became bearable for long and extensively to one. Also there are single poems (e.g. Vaughan's "They are all gone into a world of light," and Herbert's "Sweet day, so cool, so calm, so bright") which are perfect, indeed magnificent or exquisite — even *qua* poems. Yet the bulk of the poetical work of all five seems to me hopelessly disfigured as to form by their quasi-perpetual straining after some conceit, some play upon thought when that thought's seriousness demands, in good taste, the greatest possible directness, sobriety, simplicity; yet again, if one compares them with real religious English poetry, such as Keble, one finds, I think, that they contain more sheer poetry than Keble. They are more virile, somehow; I was sorry, in my last letter, that I did not make a point of your ever dear, fine father. Nothing could be more deserved than that the thought of him should have been specially with you in Canterbury; had he been frivolous and narrow-hearted you might never have come to much! Loving Uncle-Father.

CLONBOY, ENGLEFIELD GREEN, SURREY

*From letter of 7 August 1919*

My darling Gwen,

1. St. Augustine. I cannot exaggerate the gain that I think you will derive from feeding for years upon the *Confessions*. They, more than any other book excepting the Gospels and the Psalms, have taught me—and I believe they will teach you, will penetrate and will colour every tissue of your mind and heart—as to four things especially.

(i.) *Seriousness.* The average, conventional, latter-day, enlightened, etc., outlook as to moral responsibility, purity, humility, sin, is just so much childishness compared to the spirit that breathes in those deathless pages. That entire way of recording one's own or other lives, as though they were just so many crystals, or at most so many plants; as though they could not, in the given circumstances, have been other than in fact they were: all that sorry naturalism and determinism, with its cheap self-exculpation and its shallow praise (because also shallow blame) of others: all this is nobly outsoared, is obviously nowhere, in that deep manly world of St. Augustine.

(ii.) *Reality, Distinctness, Prevenience of God, our Home.* This again, how little we are recognising it! And how this fundamental fact pervades St. Augustine! It is because of this mighty fact (ii.) that fact (i.) ever taken in all its seriousness, leaves the soul rock-based, serene, unshaken; even though it wander far away from God, its Home. Yet that Home continues ready to receive it back.

(iii.) *The Church, the Community, the Tradition, the Training School of Seekers after, of Souls found by God and*

*Christ.* This great fact, overlooked nowadays as fact, and
the other two—St. Augustine had them all three in deep-
est operation—each requiring, supplementing, strength-
ening the other.

(iv.) *Our Dead—ourselves when dead.* St. Augustine is the
finest antidote to our prevalent weakness here again.
What soul ever owed more to another than Augustine to
Monica? Can there have been many souls more holy than
Monica's? And have there been many come back from
more deadly sins and errors than Augustine? Yet with all
she was, with all her saintly life and glorious death, all
still vividly before him, Augustine quietly records her
frailties and prays for her, and begs all who read him
throughout the ages to pray for her, for the forgiveness of
her sins. In this way even Monica becomes, if I may speak
in homely fashion, not a lobster-pot, but a springboard,
not a blind-alley or a terminus, but a starting-point and a
spur to seeing, willing, doing even further than her, further
than her whilst she was in this life.

2. *God.* I shall be glad if on this point you can and will
develop two distinct currents of conviction and emotion:
the *two together* will give you a deep growing faith. By all
means concentrate upon the lights that may come to you,
as it were incidentally, and as background, in and through
your prayers—of Church services, Prayer of Quiet and
Holy Communions; and leave alone definitions of Him,
and clear, reasoned articulations of your faith in, of your
conceptions of Him. Good, excellent—provided you not
only respect for others, but you interiorly reverence as indirectly but most operatively necessary for yourself, the
great positive conclusions of the greatest thinkers, theologians, saints, the great definitions of the Church concerning God. I mean learn to shrink away from the childish
attitude of Schiller, in his epigram—that he refuses to belong to any religion, because of his profound religiousness,
or of Goethe in his *Faust*—that it does not matter *what we*

*think* God to be, *what we say* of Him—that it all equally
affirms and equally denies Him. I cannot exhaustively
know, I cannot adequately define, even a daisy, still less
Puck. Still less you. Does it follow that I cannot know, in
various degrees, really know, a daisy, Puck—you—that it
does not matter how I conceive them, that *this* conception
is not ever so much more penetrating, ever so much more
true, than is *that* conception? You know Gibbon's far too
influential gibe at the Arian Controversy—that it was all a
silly squabble concerning a diphthong—as to whether
Christ was *Homo susios—same* substance with the Father—
or *Homo sousios—*of similar substance with the Father.
Gibbon thus confounded rich, far-reaching live differences,
with their ultimate reduction to technical terms. You
might as well declare that a controversy turning upon one
million pounds sterling—that presence or absence was but
a wrangle over the numerical sign—the vertical stroke—of
1. Since, on the one side, men wrangled "000,000" and, on
the other side, men wrangled "1,000,000." Of course all
great issues can intellectually be reduced to such beggar-
ly-seeming symbols; and in this reduced form they can
only appeal to those who know them in their living full-
ness and operativeness. But it is a transparent piece of
claptrap to decide off-hand, from such reductions, that
this or that one is worthy of all respect because it covers
great riches of fact, and that another deserves all con-
tempt as a mere empty formula.—My Child will then just
simply love and serve God in and through her prayers, her
joys, her sufferings—her Church and her Communions—
her children and her dear ones all—but she will *not* tilt at,
she will *not* treat lightly definitions, however dry-seeming
and abstract.

Two great laws—I am convinced they are—of and in
our little earthly lives and probation. The one fact and law
is, how unequipped are young people, say up to thirty at
the earliest, for any final negative decision as to religion. I

mean definite, institutional religion; and therefore how
heavy is the responsibility of parents and seniors if they
provoke, if they give ready occasion to, the young to any
indiscriminate revolt against such definite institutional
religion. Such seniors may have the deepest experience of
what such definite, institutional religion means in and for
*their own* lives, but they ought simultaneously to make
clear to themselves that this their own formed conviction
has been an affair of time, and that they must not presuppose it as extant in the young, or as simply transfer-
able to the young by command or even by careful teaching. This, of course, in no wise means that children and
young people should not be taught *some* religion, should
not be wisely trained in *some* religious (institutional religious) convictions and habits. It only means that at every
step you should remain conscious of the inevitable, the
right of difference between these young things and yourself—and that we will have gained a great point if they
leave your hands with only a little definite religion, but
with a sense that there may well be more in it than they
can, so far, see for themselves.

The second great fact or law of human life is that good
faith and the effects of our view and decisions (upon ourselves and others) are strikingly incommensurate. A child
is taken over a factory—in the best good faith it puts its
hand into the machinery—its good faith in no wise saves it
from its own quite sincere but entirely ignorant action. No
doubt that in more purely spiritual and moral matters,
good faith does more or less neutralise some of the effects
of inexperience, precipitation, etc.—but it does not neutralise them entirely. All this then means that we will
strive to make the young feel more and more that *sincerity*
is indeed a *one* most necessary virtue for them; but that
*docility* is quite as necessary a virtue.

Your father exemplified this so grandly in music—the
subject-matter of his special genius: he was not at all

merely himself and sincere there; but for years he kept himself at school under Dannreuther, and to the hour of his death he was definitely learning from Bach and Beethoven, Wagner — was continuing enriched and enriching a great articulate and increasingly articulated tradition. Indeed, also in religion, I love to remember how religiously-tempered he ever remained — how nobly he overflowed and left behind him in *his actual love and interests*, such books as Buckle's, which, nevertheless (owing to that early, never directly revised, inhibition and depletion), he never ceased from, now and then, praising to me. It was doubtless his most beautiful purity and love of young souls that thus kept him from being himself centrally determined by those brilliant materialists. And then, my Gwen — I look, not back, but onwards — not to what he was (even at his darling best), but to what he IS, IS in the true full life which assuredly he has already gained, or is in process of gaining.

My darling Niece-Daughter! I feel I know you, and God's purifications of you, much better since you were here those darling days. And I feel, as I felt at the moment you told me of a big, piercing fact, that you have all the materials ready to your hand of downright *holiness*. Oh, how kind and generous of God when He makes it impossible for us to become very happy unless we become very good. Bless you, Child. Pray for this old thing. I pray for you and the three.

H.

CLONBOY, ENGLEFIELD GREEN, SURREY

*18 August 1919*

My darling Gwen-Child,

I am always so glad when you can and do articulate some perplexity about one or other of the huge, rich, many-sided — not questions, but facts and laws which I try to help you to see — for thus I feel on sure ground — not only as to those great facts; but also as to your whereabouts, or your obscurity, concerning them.

I do not any more remember my exact object in telling what you have evidently remembered very accurately; but I will now take the point in (and more or less by) itself, and will make it as clear as ever I can.

You see, my Gwen, that with the all but limitless sway of *subjectivism*, especially since the eighteenth century, almost everyone nowadays, who is not deeply fed and filled by quite definite religious (institutional religious) life and convictions, thinks, if they think of truth and fact at all, of things not *given*, not found, but as things somehow projected, or created, by us (and this, all within and only for the purpose of our *human* nature and *human limitedly* human certainties and happiness). Strictly speaking, such an attitude should never speak of truth as in any sense ultimate and independent of ourselves; or of any reality as certainly existing prior to, and independently of, our affirmations of it. Such a temper of mind, if it talks of Church, of Christ, of God at all, can only talk of them as just so many "beautiful" or "interesting" ideas within your and my brain and heart — as things possibly without any reality outside of these receptacles. Such people could not ever raise the question as to *whether all three facts and realities* (as you and I hold them to be) *themselves communicate themselves to man — themselves invade his consciousness*, provided such consciousness is pure and sincere. This question, note, Dear, is distinct from the question as to whether or not Church, Christ, God, are all three true, all three real. The Roman Catholic Church — any and every Christian group or individual — who would deny, or even discriminate between, the truth, the reality, of any one of the three, would stultify itself or himself. God leads to Christ, and Christ leads to Church; and, inversely, the Church leads to Christ, and Christ leads to God. Or, better, the Church always involves Christ, and Christ always involves God; and God always involves Christ, and Christ always involves the Church.—This, Dearie, is clear enough, isn't it?

But please note (not as contradictory to this, but different to this) that when we speak thus we are speaking of the complete interconnection, the complete three-mountains-chain, as God always sees it, or some human souls here below always see it; as it is in itself, whether many or few, all or no, human souls see it. *We are not speaking as* (in this world of slow growth, of complications, and of trial, of weakness, cowardice and sin) *the situation actually stands.* Everywhere in this little "cabined" life of man we have to introduce a similar distinction between the complete *type,* as most certainly willed by God, most certainly planned by Him, and effected again and again by and with His help; *and* the incomplete, the merely inchoate *individuals*—always in all ranks of actual life the considerable majority. I believe only 5 per cent of most *flies* ever attain to their full development; yet every one of these nineteen in every twenty achieve, *as far as they go,* the type! They indicate, they imply it. With *mammals* the waste is less, but still very large—if it is right to speak of "waste" where, very possibly, life is, after all, the richer for even such inchoations. When we come to *man* we still get something similar, the many mere *beginnings* of human life—children dead before birth, or before the age of reason, idiots, the insane. Also the long centuries of barbarism. All this, note, quite independent of any personal fault, any sin, on the part of those inchoate human beings.—Well, here again we can say that so far (that is, apart from sin) the world is, after all, upon the whole richer were there no such inchoations than if it were reduced to those individuals who attain to the full human stature.

Now this great fact or law, this great *difference between type and individual, the realised ideal and the average attain-*

*ment,* runs also clearly through the manifestations of God to man, and the apprehensions by man of God and His condescensions. The Jewish religion was not false for the thirteen centuries of the pro-Christian operations; it was, for those times, God's fullest self-revelation and man's deepest apprehension of God; and this same Jewish religion can be, *is,* still the fullest religious truth for numerous individuals whom God leaves in their good faith; in their not directly requiring the fuller, the fullest, light and aid to Christianity. What is specially true of the Jewish religion is, in a lesser but still a very real degree, true of Mohammedanism, and even of Hinduism, of Parseeism, etc. It is *not* true that all religions are equally true, equally pure, equally fruitful—the differences are, on the contrary, profound. And it is our duty never to level down, never to deny or ignore, God's upward-moving self-revelation, God's *type*-religion. At the same time our ardour requires harnessing to patience, to a meek encouragement to all the smoking flax, all the broken reeds, of our earthly time and comrades, for these are God's *individuals.*

Now then, back to your precise question. The ordinary Roman Catholic scholastic textbook teaches that such good faith (not adequacy), such individual sufficiency (not type-fullness), is more operative with regard to ignorance, or even denial, of the *Christian Church,* or even of *Christ,* than with regard to denial, or even to ignorance of God. This because, after all, Church and Christ are historical, contingent facts, which require to be imparted to us, in a way, like the existence of the Emperor Augustus and the reality of the United States of America, thus at the beginning. But, no doubt, the non-Christian religions all furnish their followers with (imperfect) conceptions of God, so also with (imperfect) conceptions of Christ (Moses, Mohammed, Buddha, etc.) and imperfect conceptions of the Church (temple, mosque, etc.). Whereas God is the metaphysical absolute Reality, which is involved in, which indicates itself in, our deepest needs, thoughts and conscience. When I told you that story of Monsieur Littré, I did so, amongst other reasons, in order to indicate how careful, how non-judging, as to individuals, we should keep ourselves, even where such individuals ignore or even deny God. Yet I do think that the ordinary Roman Catholic teaching is after a very real distinction, and also that present-day ordinary cheery dismissal of all thought of responsibility, and even of guilt, in such denials, is but part and parcel of the insufferable shallowness of Naturalism.

Devoted old Uncle,
F.v.H.

CLONBOY, ENGLEFIELD GREEN, SURREY

*1 September 1919*

I want this little scribble to reach you on your starting your packing-fortnight, my very dear Niece. I want to put very shortly, what has helped myself so greatly, for now a generation.

Well—you are going to pack, pack and unpack, unpack for a fortnight. What is it that I would have you quietly set your mind and heart on, during that in itself lonesome and dreary bit of your road, Child? Why *this*, Dear! You see, all we do has a *double-relatedness*. It is a link or links of a chain that stretches back to our birth and on to our death. It is part of a long train of cause and effect, of effect and cause, in your own chain of life—this chain variously intertwisted with, variously affecting, and affected by, numerous other chains and other lives. It is certainly your duty to do quietly your best, that these links may help on your own chain and those other chains, by packing well, by being a skilful packer.

Yes, but there is also, all the time, another, a far deeper, a most darling and inspiring relation. Here, you have no slow succession, but you have each single act, each single moment joined directly to GOD—Himself not a chain, but one Great Simultaneity. True, certain other acts, at other moments, will be wanted, of a kind more intrinsically near to God—Prayer, Quiet, Holy Communion. Yet not even those other acts could unite you as closely to God as can do this packing, if and when the packing is the duty of certain moments, and if, and as often as, the little old daughter does this her packing with her heart and intention turned to God her Home, if she offers her packing as her service, that service which is perfect liberty.

Not even a soul already in Heaven, not even an angel or archangel, can take your place there; for what GOD wants, what GOD will love to accept, in those Herst rooms, in those packing days, and from your packing hands, will be just this little packing performed by the little niece in those little rooms. Certainly it has been mainly through my realising this doctrine a little, and through my poor little self-exercising in it, that I have got on a bit, and Gwen will get on faster than I have done with it. You understand, Dear? At one moment packing; at another, silent adoration in church; at another, dreariness and unwilling drift; at another, the joys of human affections given and received; at another, keen, keen suffering of soul, of mind, in an apparent utter loneliness; at another, external acts of religion; at another, death itself. All these occupations, every one, can, ought, and will be, each when and where, duty, reason, conscience, necessity—GOD calls for it—it will all become the means and instruments of loving, of transfiguration, of growth for your soul, and of its beatitude. But it is for GOD to choose these things, their degrees, combinations, successions; and it is for Gwen, just simply, very humbly, very gently and peacefully, to follow that leading.

*Letters to a Niece*

*Per Crucem ad Lucem.*[1]
Loving old Uncle,
H.

CLONBOY, ENGLEFIELD GREEN, SURREY

*17 September 1919*

Well, now, my darling Gwen, here is my letter for your restarting in Salisbury. I will attempt to make two, more or less new, points—very important discriminations—very clear for you, after first getting two immediate practical details out of the way.

I want you, then, carefully to study all the remaining Latin (Roman) Christian books I have given or lent you in the last packets. Tell me when you are getting to the end of this study (the little Tertullian and the Swete at least twice, please!), and I will get quite ready for the first packet of Greek books—classical (Pagan) Greek books first—on the same scale as that we did the Latin books on.

And the second detail is your proposed visit to Vicarage Gate—excellent idea! Hillie and I get back there on Monday next, 22 September. I have to speak at a Birmingham little private meeting—all my hearers clerics—on Monday, 27 October, and I ought to keep at least ten days free before, for preparation. Your Aunt Mary has a lady friend, who has asked herself till about 2 October. As soon after this 2 October that you can manage, say, three nights with us, the better, as the weather will then be more likely to favour our getting our talks in Kensington Gardens than later on. If you came by lunch-time, and left by an afternoon train, that too would add to our time in common. Let Aunt Mary or Hillie or me know, some time pretty soon, Gwen!

---

[1] Latin: Through the Cross to the Light.

50

## Baron Friedrich von Hügel

Now for my points:

1. It is quite possible (it is certainly much the more common state of soul) that your now deep and living sense of religion is making non-religious subjects more or less insipid to you—that you are feeling it rather a bore to concentrate upon Homer and Pindar, after Tertullian and the *Confessions*. But if this is so, or if it comes on later on, I want you, my Gwen, *carefully to ignore and vigorously to react against this mentality*. If there is one danger for religion—if there is any one plausible, all-but-irresistible trend which, throughout its long rich history, has sapped its force, and prepared the most destructive counter-excesses, it is just that—that allowing the fascinations of Grace to deaden or to ignore the beauties and duties of Nature. What *is* Nature? I mean all that, in its degree, is beautiful, true, and good, in this many-levelled world of the one stupendously rich God? Why, Nature (in this sense) is the expression of the God of Nature; just as Grace is the expression of the God of Grace. And not only are *both* from God, and to be loved and honoured as His: but they have been created, they are administered and moved, by God, as *closely inter-related parts of one great whole*—of the full and vivid knowledge and service of Him and happiness of ourselves. No Grace without the substrata, the occasion, the material, of Nature; and (in the individuals called to the realisation of the type) no Nature without Grace. Do you fully grasp, my Gwen, what I am driving at? That I want you, just because you long for religion, to continue to cultivate, to cultivate more carefully and lovingly, also the interests, the activities, that are not directly religious. And this, not simply because, "Why, of course, we must eat our dinner; of course, we must have our little relaxations"; but, much more, because, without these not directly religious interests and activities, you—however slowly and unperceivedly—lose the material for Grace to work in and on. When we come to do the Church history

of the Middle Ages, and of the Renaissance, etc., I shall be able to point out to you, on a huge scale, this great principle either fructifying all or sterilising all. Meanwhile, practise, practise it, Gwen; and keep it up, long after I have gone! *Hardly any woman works her religion thus*; but then, too, how thin and abstract, or how strained and unattractive, the religion of most women becomes, owing to this their elimination of religion's materials and divinely intended tensions!

2. Hardly distinguishable in theory, yet rather different in practice, is the other point I want you carefully to watch. I have so much insisted upon *the Church* in my recommendations that it may look inconsistent if I warn you against Church societies, Church newspapers—the little Churchinesses which, I should think, must be fairly frequent in your cathedral town—yet, my Gwen! just this, the equivalent of just this, has been perhaps my longest, subtlest difficulty and temptation, ever since, through God's mercy, the Church took me, and I gave myself to the Church. It was only when I was forty that this trouble and uncertainty ceased—again owing to light from and through a saintly leader. I never have gained the bigger lights on myself, except that way. To love Holy Communion, yet tactfully, unironically, to escape from all Eucharistic Guilds, etc.; to care for God's work in the world especially in and through Christianity, and yet (again quite silently, with full contrary encouragement to others who are helped by such literature) never opening a Church paper or magazine; and so on, and so on: what a pushing forward and a sudden inhibiting back all this seems to be!

Yet, if you are made at all like myself—what safety, what expansion, will be yours! This, though, only if you have your life full of good, wholesome not technically religious interests; and if these non-religious interests are more and more penetrated, warmed, widened, sweetened by the purest, humblest, most self-oblivious, homely heroism of super-nature—of Grace in the full sense of the word. Such a life will also greatly help you in keeping free from what might make you an unnecessary stumbling-block to other not yet religiously awake souls; and this without the least indifference or sorry "naturalising" on your part. At forty I learnt this; at forty or so, my Gwen, learn you this also.

I need not say that neither 1 nor 2 are of any obligation for you. They are only suggestions for you to watch and to see whether, and how, they fit you. If you cannot get forward in this fashion, by all means get on in the other way. I only want to clear away every possible half-notion that to love God, Christ, Church dearly, it is necessary for everyone (hence also for you) to be *churchy*. But again, Gwen, humility, consideration, patience: encouraging of others to become quite different from ourselves; all this can alone render the kind of independence I mean, safe, because creaturely, and the isolation not fundamental or ultimate, but only one concerned with middle things, with means and afflictions.

Am now weary. God bless you, Child. Be faithful, and He will sweeten to you, in the long run, all things, even bitter death itself.

Loving old,
Uncle.

VICARAGE GATE

*23 September 1919*

My darling Gwen,
Your interesting letter, awaiting my return here yesterday, raises important points which I will *consider* with you in a letter a little later on (and when you turn up here for one night), on 8 October. Better that than nothing!

But I must at once make the following suggestions to you as to the five books I send you to-day. Your first Greek packet. They are all your property — except one volume — Bury's *History of Greece.* You can, if you like, begin at once on Homer. But I think it will be better to take the three histories first, and only then the Homer and the Hesiod. But in any case you should read the histories in the order: (1) Bury, (2) Gilbert Murray, (3) Croiset; and the texts in the order: (1) Iliad, (2) Odyssey, (3) Hesiod.

Now as to these six volumes singly:

(1) *Bury.* I wish I could have found another one volume, as recent and (for surface matters) as competent a history of Greece, by some other more believing and spiritual writer. For Bury is a clever, smart, shallow thing — is growing it more and more, and aggressively irreligious as well. But this book is very much up-to-date as to excavations — the maps and illustrations are excellent — and in it he is not so rampantly doctrinaire as he has since become. Perhaps one careful reading with notes taken from it will be enough — keeping the book by you for further occasional use.

(2) *Murray.* Hardly, even he, a very deep, rich soul; but distinctly better than Bury — and has a wonderful penetration in the literature as such — I would certainly read him, most carefully, at least twice.

(3) *Croiset.* You will feel the charm of these Frenchmen; read it twice. Have got their larger five-volume *History*; and could at any time lend you this or that — or all the volumes.

(4) *Iliad.* I think this translation is the best for understanding Homer. Pray read and re-read it all, and compare the parts in the Æneid with the corresponding parts here — a very educative study.

(5) *Odyssey.* I send the translation of that cranky genius — S. Butler — because it so wonderfully hits off the homey tone of the original — and the maps, pictures, notes,

are all most suggestive. But, of course, his contention that
the author was a woman is sheer moonshine—not very
unlike Harnack's contention that Priscilla (with Aquila's
collaboration) wrote the Epistle to the Hebrews. But re-
read the Odyssey and compare carefully corresponding
parts (very numerous and lengthy) in the Æneid

(6) *Hesiod.* Introduction and *Works and Days* at least
twice—remainder once—compare *Works and Days* carefully with Virgil's *Georgics.*
Devoted old Uncle,
F.v.H.

13 VICARAGE GATE, W. 8

*6 October 1919*

My darling Gwen,
I write to-day, hoping that this (now the strike is over)
may reach you to-morrow—on the first anniversary of
your dear father's death. I often and often think of him;
indeed he, just as you yourself, child, are in my poor
prayers thrice every day. And I love to think that, if he, in
that great life beyond, is allowed to know what happens
here below to his youngest, he is glad and grateful for
your deep growth during this year thus just gone by. This
growth has assuredly preserved, and only still further
deepened, the noble good—all the touching purity and
generosity—he taught you and he exemplified to you, indeed which, in a true sense, he gave you with his blood.

I want to write now, also, because, since you cannot
come just now (very naturally, though I am truly sorry), I
should like to make some remarks upon quite a number
of practical points or of questions raised by you since last
I wrote.

1. As to the practical points:
(i.) Much frequentation of the cathedral. You know
well, how greatly I love this for you. Yet there is one

55

warning I would give you, and would beg you to bear in mind. *Do not overdo it*: I mean, do not take your utter fill, while the attraction is thus strong.

If we want our fervour to last, we must practise moderation even in our prayer, even in our Quiet. And certainly it is perseverance in the spiritual life, on and on, across the years and the changes of our moods and trials, health and environment: it is this that supremely matters. And you will, Gwen, add greatly to the probabilities of such perseverance, if you will get into the way (after having settled upon the amount of time that will be wise for you to give to the cathedral, or your Prayer of Quiet in general) of keeping a little even beyond this time, when you are dry; and a little short of this time when you are in consolation. You see why, don't you? — Already the Stoics had the grand double rule: *abstine et sustine,* "abstain and sustain," i.e. moderate thyself in things attractive and consoling, persevere, hold out, in things repulsive and desolating. There is nothing God loves better, or rewards more richly, than such double self-conquest as this! Whereas, all those who heedlessly take their glut of pleasant things, however sacred these things may be, are in grave danger of soon outliving their fervour, even if they do not become permanently disgusted.

(ii.) As to *Churchy* people, I did not, of course, mean devotedly Christian people, lovers of the Church, who work these loves into a large thoughtfulness ....

(iii.) As to Bury's *History*: please, Dear, write your name in it, and keep it as a further gift from me: it will be very useful for frequent reference in most of your further readings of Greek things. And, Child, try, by very frequent looking at the coin illustrations, to connect the chief Greek cities with their coins. It is in that way that the geography of ancient Greece sticks in my head. And dull as geography, and still more chronology, are, when taken simply by themselves — yet without them — without a clear framework of time and space in which to place and to remember the facts, external or interior, of the history, you will never remember the facts, and hence you will never be able yourself to reason upon, to apply the history. Let the coins help you very largely!

2. As to questions:

(i.) Shakespeare's *Macbeth*. I think you are right, and that *there* is a truly Christian penetration and estimate. To-day week I will send you, on long loan, a *glorious* book: Bradley's *Shakesperean Tragedy: Hamlet, Macbeth, Othello, Lear*. You will love it, I am sure. It is a book really worthy of its subject.

(ii.) Shorthouse's *John Inglesant*. I must say I feel that book to have but *one* (a truly great) greatness, as against three very bad faults—faults which, I must confess, continue to spoil the pleasure I might otherwise find in it. The book, then, I think, has one perception, or, rather, an instinct stronger than the author is himself aware of—I mean an all-penetrating sense of the massiveness, the awful reality, of the spiritual life within the Roman Catholic Church. This that he thus sees, is assuredly a fact, and a huge fact; but it is a fact unknown, or turned away from, or minimised by the large majority even of religious Englishmen. And I really believe that the undoubtedly great fascination of this book for so many serious souls is just this, its all-pervading sense of that very certain but very largely unknown fact. But then I feel that to one who, like myself, has lived within, has lived and been redeemed and been formed by that great life in that great Church, that discovery of Shorthouse is no discovery: if anything, such an one is somewhat irritated that something to him so massively plain, should—the discovery of it—stamp a book as quite *sui generis*. And then, against that strength of the book stand, I think, three great—even if smaller, weaknesses. (1) The book, the man's style, indeed mind, are *precious*—surely as much so as is Pater's *Marius*. All

57

that is turned and re-turned, is cooked—to my taste to weariness. (2) The central figure and fate in the book— Molinos and his end—are far from certainly what they are painted here. *Possible* it is that Molinos was innocent; I have studied the case very carefully, and have said so in print. But there is no certainty; and much—too much— mysticism and moral depravity have certainly gone together in not a few other cases. (3) The underlying doctrine of the book is very lopsided, indeed it is false. All through a Quaker indifference to the visible, to Forms, to History— to the Body in Time and Space—is actively at work. Yet nothing is being more clearly re-proved, quite independently of the old institutions, by modern psychology, than that that independence is only possible in a world saturated with the results of dependence. Mysticism, in all religions, always comes long after those religions have won and trained the soul by their historic happenednesses, by their close contact with time and space. We shall find this, my Gwen, later on, with the Ancient Greek, the Indian, the Jewish, the Mohammedan, the Christian religions. And to think like Shorthouse is historic ingratitude of a high degree. I find that, throughout his book, those that insist strongly on institutions and that fear or oppose more or less pure Mysticism, are all, in so far, worldlings, power-lovers, Pharisees, etc.! Stuff and nonsense: I *know* that this is a clumsy, false analysis; although, of course, there are worldlings amongst the strong institutionalists, as there are fanatics or moral decadents amongst the "exquisite" mystics.

3. Dean Colet. Yes, he is a very attractive personality, and Seebohm's book is a good book. But I have changed— I have had to change much as to those Renaissance Catholic reformers these last ten years. My ideal used to be Sir Thomas More. I still, of course, admit their greatness; and I hold still, with all my heart, that *that* Reform would have been far better than the Protestant violences

which supplanted it. But I now have found in detail how profoundly ignorant, how bigoted, were all these men, as to the Middle Ages—they lumped these latter indiscriminately together, as just one long—six or seven centuries or more—of utter barbarism and contemptible puerilities. Dante and Aquinas, Anselm, Bernard, the Poverello: barbarians! What a notion! The fact is, certainly—we are all coming to know it well now—that these men came at the fag-end of some five generations of Iron Middle Ages, of their dissolution; and they were too disgusted, too impatient, too much blinded by the new light and lights, to pierce through those 150 years, back to the Golden Middle Ages. The Golden Middle Age is the culmination, so far, of the Christian spirit as a world force and a world outlook; and compared with its greatest figures just named, even More and Colet, Fisher and Erasmus, are thin and literary indeed. This too, Sweet, you will be shown in detail later on.

Now I will have to be pretty silent till October is at an end; have to incubate my address at Birmingham on 27 October. Grand if you could come here soon after.

Loving old Uncle,
H.

13 VICARAGE GATE, KENSINGTON

*From letter of All Saints' Eve, 1919*

My darling Niece-Child,

Here, at last, I come to speak to you again on paper—the work, the getting to, and the resting from, Birmingham have, till now, prevented me. But I was very glad to get that sweet little letter of yours, before starting off from this huge Babylon for that also very big place. I myself felt, once off, that I was attempting a great deal. Yet it all went off, I think, quite well. My two forenoons there I spent in the really beautiful Art Galleries—I enclose photo

post card of one of the pictures for my darling Gwen. But
how much of the art of not thirty years ago, or a little beyond — Leighton, Burne-Jones especially — has already died
without repair, and why? Because it was *precious*, un-
moral, at bottom un-, even anti-Christian (in the widest
sense of the word). One feels it affiliated to moral un-
wholesomeness ....

Strange it is, but a fact, that *human* studies should
more incline men to religion than *natural* studies; strange
because the difficulties against religion are almost con-
fined to precisely the human range. The fact is, doubtless,
that religion thrives, not by the absence of difficulties, but
by the presence, by its offer and proof of powers not pro-
curable otherwise; and that the need for these powers, and
the evidence for the operation of their forces, only arises
clearly at the human level.

...

Gwen, look up, look up with me, to-morrow! Oh, what
a glorious, touching company! It is the feast of every heroic soul, every heroic act inspired by God since man began on earth. Sweet, how our little earthly years are fleeing
by. Pindar called our life "the dream of a shadow." Yet in
it, and through it, if we but watch and pray, and work
and suffer, and rest in God our Home, we can find Eternity; that will never pass away. Pray for your loving old,
    Uncle-Father.

13 VICARAGE GATE, KENSINGTON W. 8

*3 December 1919*

My Gwen-Child,

Here, then, is *Eternal Life*. I would advise your first
reading up to the end of page 120, twice. Then, pages 303
to end, twice. And only then the far more difficult pages
121-302, also twice. Unless I greatly err, you will learn a
considerable amount, provided you understand the tech-

nicalities as they occur. I did not choose the title, or even my subject; but you will find friends, already known, in these pages—St. Augustine, Huvelin, etc., not to speak of the Psalms and the New Testament—I wrote the thing praying; read it as written, Child!

I am sorry you are finding the Croiset so dry. I see why—my fault. Those two brothers wrote a delightful not dry, *History of Greek Literature*, in the five volumes—have got it. But I stupidly forgot how all abridgments are, almost always, dry as sawdust! So do not, Sweet, force yourself to read it through.

Your new packet is getting ready nicely. But the Herodotus is reprinting just now; and I have not yet spotted the Bury on the Greek historians. But I have a good little book on Pindar ready; Pindar translated by Ernest Myers, and a fine selection of translations from the *Greek Anthology*—if you don't love the latter well, you will show a patch of insensibility on your brain.

I well understand how delightful your father's Eton diaries must be; they will form an important part of the *Life*, no doubt. I love to note, Dear, that the same kind of spontaneous intelligence for, and thirst after music, and the same assumption that such intelligence and thirst are, must be, universal, are with you, his daughter, in reference to religion. Thekla has been telling me how marked she found a trait of genuine contemplation in you, Sweet. Well, it is all God's work; we will think of Him and love Him ever more and more; and we will bear as patiently as ever we can our loneliness in these respects. We will never feel badly lonely, if we keep expanding our direct knowledge of living lovers of God by a vivid realisation of the love of him borne in the hearts of souls now in the beyond.

I am so glad you loved the Huvelin: you will have noticed everywhere in him that tenderness in austerity and that austerity in tenderness, which is the very genius of Christianity.

Must not scribble on to-day. Have started studying for
my book, and I require oceans of rest in between.
Loving old Uncle-Father,
H.

*2 January 1920*

My darling Gwen-Child,
I had counted upon writing my first 1920 letter to you;
but, alas, strict duty intervened, and forced me to write to
other three people instead. But I want you to look upon
this scribble as though written on New Year's Day itself.

I want, then, to wish you a very rich, deep, true,
straight and simple growth in the love of God, accepted
and willed gently but greatly, *at the daily, hourly, cost of
self.* I have to try my little old best more than ever at this,
now; for I find that any and all brooding or sulking or
useless self-occupation—any pride or vanity at once dis-
turbs or dries up my incubation-work. Professor James
Ward and I agreed, one day, that nothing in philosophy,
still more in religion, should ever be attempted in and with
the first clearness (what, e.g., journalists are content with,
and have to be content with), but in and with the *second
clearness*, which only comes after that first cheery clarity
has gone, and has been succeeded by a dreary confusion
and obtuseness of mind. Only this second clearness, rising
up, like something in no wise one's own, from the depths
of one's subconsciousness—only this is any good in such
great matters. And this process is costly, humiliating, and
very easily disturbed by rubbishy self-occupations.

I am so glad you are trying to work the *Imitation* into
your life: it is the only way to read it which is really worthy of what itself is so intensely alive. Now *there* is a book
written as should be all religious books; they should be the
quintessence of a long experience and fight in suffering

and self-transformation. Also the twenty Huvelin sayings — they sprang straight from a life penetrated by God and the deepest love of Him. I will, a little later on, copy out for you another twenty sayings — they are all, please God, at work within me; and how happy, if they can get to work in the Niece-child also!

As to my *Apocalyptic Element* keep it as long as you feel re-reading it can help you. I have two or three other papers which may also be of use to you. But, you see, with religious reading I always feel the situation is different from more ordinary reading. I mean that religious reading should always be select, slow, ruminating, and given to comparatively few books or papers. So we will, when you are again ready, get on with our Greek things — plenty of *them* — and, alongside, and behind them all, will be our few deepest readings, full of prayer, full of self-humiliation, full of gentle attempts gently to will whatever suffering God may *kindly* send us. A Jesuit novice once told me, with kindling countenance, how grand he had found the practice of *at once* meeting suffering with joy. God alone can help us succeed in this; but what, Child, is Christianity, if it be not something like that?

Loving old,
Uncle-Father.


*From letter of 17 February 1920 – Shrove Tuesday*

My darling Child,

I want this letter to reach you on Ash Wednesday, when we all start Lent, because there is one little practice I should like to dwell upon for a minute, in case you have not yet waked up to it, or that you require, perhaps, a little encouragement in it. I mean the practice of some little voluntary renunciation. I know well, of course, my Gwen, how much vague and airy wisdom oozes out of the comfortable and hallow modern mind about this. But then you see, we have the *little* (!) examples of the Baptist in the wilderness, with his wild honey and locusts meal; Our Lord's Fast of forty days; St. Paul's mastery of his body; and really, without a break, the asceticism of all the great saints. I say this not to suggest anything special in your food, sleep or dress; and as to the amount of church, half an hour a day will be enough, and it would be unwise to add to it, even in Lent. But I am thinking of something without thinking *what* — that would correspond, say, to my not buying my books for myself during Lent. Depend upon it, such little self-checks — checks on good propensions, and checks self-imposed — where they spring from love, really feed love. They are good things and still useful to your spiritual growth.

Loving old,

Father-Uncle.

### 13 VICARAGE GATE

*20 February 1920*

My darling Child,

You will by now have already got those two big tomes of mine.[2] May you find sufficient that you really understand, or can get to understand, to make your study of them spiritually fruitful. The book has been out of print some four years now; but this copy is really (barring the wrappers) still quite fresh; it was quite uncut-open yesterday; it is I who cut it open for you, Sweet! Bishop Gore, who has been very kind about the book, pointed out several grave defects in it. That the style is often heavy, sometimes slipshod; that there is too much of quotation, or semi-quotation in it; and that the narration portion is without any narrative charm. I am sure he is right about

---

[2]*The Mystical Element in Religion.*

all three points. But I feel him wrong about a fourth objection of his: that I ought to have taken a fully normal saint, like St. Teresa, and not a person so difficult to know, so unusual, and more or less out of the way even in her natural character, as is this Fiesca. He is wrong, because I wanted precisely such a figure for my special purposes. I wanted a heroic Christian who was almost a Neo-Platonist, an Institutional who, in some ways, hung loosely on institutions; a deep thinker beset with much psycho-physical disturbance, etc. Similarly Professor Boyce-Gibson was, I feel, mistaken, when he wanted the book to have finished—the first volume—with the death of Ettore Vernazza. He did not see that I was well aware of the inferiority, at least in charm, of Battista to Catherine, to Ettore. What then? I was not aiming at a work of art, but at taking in as much as possible of real life—to show very original and exquisite spirituality having to live on largely in this rough world, to get somewhat conventionalified to suit the array of even very good people. Of course, that Bishop Gore and Professor Boyce-Gibson did not see these two motives of mine in the book itself, proves how little an artist in words the old Uncle is!

I think you would find the Appendix at end of Volume I too dry and hard for you. But I hope that you will really care for, and learn from, the Introduction and the whole of Volume II It is chapter ii (in the Introduction) that has had much the most of the appreciation accorded to the book; but, for myself, I feel as though Volume II was the best of the whole.

My Sweet, you were thoroughly right about Richard—his unripeness for Tiele—I am sure I often make that sort of mistake for the young.

Your simile, your example of the two clearances in musical execution is capital. So glad of it, too, because it shows you are getting well into your violining again. Am surrounded by the middle state—the obscurity and muddle—as regards my book. One must just work on and hope and pray. The God of light will help us.

H.

13 VICARAGE GATE, W. 8

*From letter of 5 March 1920*

My darling Gwen-Child,

I was so sorry that you had a headache when you wrote me that last note. Mind you do not use your head on any concentrated work when you are like that ....

But I was very pleased that somehow you are able to resume the systematic non-religious reading. I was a little astonished at this, having thought, regretfully, that your life had really become too full for such reading. This notion of mine explains that I was not, on the receipt of your note, ready with further Greek books for just this stage of your reading.

I wondered too, for a moment, whether you had not possibly forgotten, or had not yet explored, the *other* Pindar book I sent you. I got you this later booklet, just because I knew well how much the reading of Pindar becomes really enjoyable, the background of which you speak. I thought this booklet would supply this environment; anyhow I at once ordered for you an excellent book, *The Athletic Festivals of Ancient Greece*. But I learn it is out of print. I have now, however, gone one better and ordered you Whitley's *Companion to Greek Studies*, which will not only illustrate Pindar for you, but also the Historians, and the Dramatists, indeed the Philosophers also, I hope. I think I can count on having this fine book on Monday ....

The packet will contain three further books:

*a. The Extent Odes of Pindar*, translated by Ernest Myers; a scholarly piece of work which I should like you to read, ode for ode, each after the translation of Sandys.

3. ... a *Guide to British Museum Greek and Roman Life*.

4. ... a *Guide to the Principal Gold and Silver Coins of the Ancients, 700 B.C. to A.D. 1.*

When we have fully and repeatedly assimilated Pindar (mind you also read André Brémond's article on him) we will move on to the Greek Historians. I shall want you to get to first love Herodotus. We will do him in a leisurely, sun-basking way which alone befits this leisurely genial soul.

I am sure that when, say twenty years hence, you look back upon your life, you will specially thank God for this double current I have tried to establish in your mind and soul. The current directly religious—this very pure in quality and genially costly; the current not directly religious, this also very large and deep—a great bucket of pure water into which to drop drops of the purest religious wine. This greatly helps us to escape all reactions.

Loving old Uncle,

H.

13 VICARAGE GATE, KENSINGTON, W.

*17 March 1920*

My darling Child,

I do not at all like these bad headaches of yours, and the suspicion that perhaps it is the fiddling that causes them. I should indeed grieve if you had to give up what so uniquely expresses your true self. I am comforting myself by hoping that, even if it really is the violining, it is *that* only in the sense that you are paying for the acclimatising of your nerves, etc., to this large, now new, life; and that, by dodging the headaches and wisely persevering in between them, you may be able to end by adapting your physical conditions to it—or again you might have to reduce the playing for a while, say, to two hours a day, instead of four hours. I hope that, in any case, my little old Gwen daughter will strive elastically to manage the fiddling after all. There is certainly a great art in managing one's nervous energy. I have myself, all my life, had to coax, and by various circumvendifuges, get my work out of my restive kittle-cattle machinery.

Glad Olivia does the types of Greek coins with you — I have no ambition for you to take up numismatics generally — whole tracts of that country seem to me hardly more soul-feeding than postage stamps. It is the *Greek* coins that really are educative — not as coins — but *Greek*, as part of that marvellous people's artistic creations. Had Richard here on Monday — looking forward to having him for a night soon. I feel you treat that very promising lad *exactly* rightly.

Your loving old,
Father.

13 VICARAGE GATE, W. 8

*26 March 1920*

My darling Gwen-Child,

A hundred, a thousand welcomes, of nature and of grace, of the sweet spring country, of the future delightful garden, of the spacious, almost empty, bedroom — full, full, Gwen, of the thought, the presence, the real presence of the living God, and of the little old church so nearby, which will always welcome you to its sacred coolness and dimness, and remind you of God's condescensions in the Incarnation and Holy Eucharist! Welcome, too, from those nice, ten workmen — such an excellent experience for those three! Welcome, too, from those said three — how soon all three will be there, and how soon after they will have come really to feel this home at last, all the more so since they will themselves help to make it all really homey! Welcome, too, from Edward Talbot, the cleric who has helped you so much and also will so much care to see your *settlement*.

I am so pleased, too, that you have evidently got fully bitten by Pindar, that that grandly clean and religious mind is colouring your own. Bravo!

I received back from you, all right, the Gardner *Types of Greek Coins*—the Butcher, the catalogue of Greek gems (glad you admired that wonderful Augustus cameo!), and André Brémond's raper [*sic*] on Pindar, and my two articles on Troeltsch (I expect the poor little Gwen found these really too hard to read). By all means keep those other four papers of mine yet awhile.

I spoke on Tuesday evening last (23rd) to some sixty students from all the English, Scotch, Welsh and Irish universities and chief colleges. The Executive Council of the Christian Student Movement—very eager, cultivated, religious young people. I spoke for forty-five minutes on "Responsibility and Religious Belief." Now I am busy writing out suggestions and criticisms for a new sketch of that striking Sikh convert to Christianity, Sadhu-Sundar-Singh. My chief desideratum here is that he should come to realise not only the utility, but the strict necessity, of definite Church appurtenance and ecclesiastical subordination. You see, a month after his conversion at sixteen, he felt called to, and took, the vow of the Sadhu life—the Indian ascetical, celibate, poor, wandering life—which he now took as that of a Christian preaching friar. He has faithfully practised this to now (twenty-nine). But even the slight Church appurtenance which sprang from his baptism by the Anglican Metropolitan of India, and his six months' study in an Anglican theological college, with a preaching licence granted him at the end—even that he soon repudiated—to the great joy of the Nonconformist individualist missionaries of India. I am trying to show how crude, how without solid Christian precedents is such a monasticism, with such a sheer aloofness from every Church organisation. I am trying to drive home St. Teresa's magnificent rule for all her own life and for that of her nuns to this day—that she believed herself to have received very real direct revelations, and that she hoped her nuns might receive the same. But that *never* had she allowed herself or were they to allow themselves, under the apparent suggestion of any revelation, to decide *anything* concerning their duties, work, appurtenances, dependants. On the contrary, the genuineness of the revelations, or at least the right use made of them, would always have to be measured by the *increased* obedience, self-oblivion, love of enemies, suffering—death, of the recipient of such favours.

God bless you, child.

H.

From Easter Monday Letter

*5 April 1920*

My darling Gwen,

I was so glad to get your first Old Rectory letter of 30 March. But first let me say that I have purposely waited till we should have got through these every year newly wonderful Church days—so as to be able to refer to the entire prism of many-coloured fact and emotion—which only thus together give us the true Christian reality and life. The great fact, and even the commemoration of, Good Friday, would, alone, be too austere, too heartbreaking; the great fact, and even just the feast of Easter, if alone—even if they had followed upon Our Lord's Hidden Life, or even His Preaching, but without the Passion and its commemoration, would not have drained the Cup—the bitter Cup—of the possibilities of earthly human life and earthly human interconnection to the dregs. Good Friday and Easter Sunday, the two together, each requiring the other, and we all requiring both—only this twin fact gives us Christianity, where suffering holds a necessary place, but never the place of the end, always only of the means.

## Baron Friedrich von Hügel

My great Troeltsch always marvels anew at that *unique* combination effected by Christianity—so earnest and so *un*rigoristic—so expansive and so full of suffering without morbidness, and of joy without sentimentality. We will all, please God, see this more and more every year, that these bitter-sweet, contraction-expansion, sacrifice serenity, great days come round.

...

Oh, how, next to one's prayers and the practice of the Presence of God, one's work, my absorption in the mornings in my book—its immediate preparation and composition, helps one to limit, to ignore and bear one's load.

I am now deep in section I of the body of the book, but dare not yet write any of this till I see more clearly, more vividly, the main points and lines of my position. It is *Kant* especially I have to master, as to contend with—the section on him in *Eternal Life* may have given you some fair notion of him.

13 VICARAGE GATE, KENSINGTON W. 8

*21 April 1920*

Here at last, my Gwen-child, I come to my scribbling to you! I have four letters of yours—three of them long. But I think they give me chiefly one big subject-matter for consideration—the stress of dryness and darkness and what to do then. I know—oh, well, well—what that means. And I do not doubt that with your special temperament, such times must be peculiarly trying. But—mark this well, Child—*irreplaceably profitable*. If you but gently persevere through them, you will come out at the other end of the gloom, sooner or later, into ever deeper, tenderer day.

Let me give you three images, all of which have helped me on along "many a flinty furlong." At eighteen I learnt from Father Raymond Hecking, that grandly interior-minded Dominican, that I certainly could, with God's grace, give myself to Him and strive to live my life long with Him and for Him. But that this would mean winning and practising much desolation—that I would be climbing a mountain where, off and on, I might be enveloped in mist for days on end, unable to see a foot before me. Had I noticed how mountaineers climb mountains? How they have a quiet, regular, short step—on the level it looks petty; but then this step they keep up, on and on, as they ascend, whilst the inexperienced townsman hurries along, and soon has to stop, dead beat with the climb. That such an expert mountaineer, when the thick mists come, halts and camps out under some slight cover brought with him, quietly smoking his pipe, and moving on only when the mist has cleared away.

Then in my thirties I utilised another image, learnt in my Jesuit Retreats. How I was taking a long journey on board ship, with great storms pretty sure ahead of me; and how I must now select, and fix in my little cabin, some few but entirely appropriate things—a small trunk fixed up at one end, a chair that would keep its position, tumbler and glass that would do ditto: all this, simple, strong, and selected throughout in view of stormy weather. So would my spirituality have to be chosen and cultivated especially in view of "dirty" weather.

And lastly, in my forties another image helped me— they all three are in pretty frequent use still! I am travelling on a camel across a huge desert. Windless days occur, and then all is well. But hurricanes of wind will come, unforeseen, tremendous. What to do then? It is very simple, but it takes much practice to do well at all. Dismount from the camel, fall prostrate face downwards on the sand, covering your head with your cloak. And lie thus, an hour, three hours, half a day: the sandstorm will go, and you will arise, and continue your journey as if nothing had happened. The old Uncle has had many, many such sandstorms. How immensely useful they are!

## Baron Friedrich von Hügel

You see, whether it be great cloud-mists on the mountain-side, or huge, mountain-high waves on the ocean, or blinding sandstorms in the desert: there is each time one crucial point—to form no conclusions, to make no decisions, to change nothing during such crises, and especially at such times, not to force any particularly religious mood or idea in oneself. To turn gently to other things, to maintain a vague, general attitude of resignation—to be very meek, with oneself and with others: the crisis goes by, thus, with great fruit. What is a religion worth which costs you nothing? What is a sense of God worth which would be at your disposal, capable of being comfortably elicited when and where you please? It is far, far more God who must hold us, than we who must hold Him. And we get trained in these darknesses into that sense of our impotence without which the very presence of God becomes a snare.

As to your feeling the facts of life and of religion complicated—*that* would be, I expect, in any oppressive way, only during such desolations. Yet I want to note this point for you—viz. that though I believe your *Confessions* and *Imitation* (with Psalms and New Testament), and the Church Service, do not strain you, nor, I think, my letters written specially for yourself, I am not at all sure of my writings in this respect. I mean that they are the writings of, I believe a masculine mind—that they contain far more sheer thinking than is suited to a woman—even a woman with as rarely much intellect as yourself, Child. This is why I was slow to give or to lend you my writings. Yet I did so, because I want you to feel that there is also much hard thinking, much unpettifying of the great lesson which God's world and work convey if we can and do front them fairly. I wanted you, even in times of temptation, to feel the realities you were called to, perhaps straining at times —even apparently mere illusions—but not cramping, not petty. You can thus settle quietly into your little cabin

73

with the huge billows buffeting you, the ship: their size
has not been minimised: they *are* huge: well, God is in the
storm as in the calm! But, of course, I am deeply glad the
sunshine and calm are back again. And certainly these,
and these at their utmost, are intended for our eventual
life!

> Par passage pénible
> Passons à port plaisant,[3]

carved a prisoner on to the wall of his cell, during his long
imprisonment in the White Tower of the Tower of London.
*That* is just it; both are true, both are facts: the *pénible* of
the *passage*, and the *plaisant*—oh, its grand expanse—of
the *port*.

As to Olivia's English literature—I enclose the list of
*Selections* I was thinking of—from the 1913 catalogue of
the Clarendon Press; they will be costing now, not four-
pence but sixpence, I expect. Am so glad I was made to
learn a lot by heart as a boy; Olivia might do the same
from out of these excellent *Selections*.

Mr. Clement Webb is to preside at my address at Oxford on 16 May: so that I shall be sitting under an old and
very tactful friend. My book preparations are getting on,
and help me to forget the financial trials.

13 VICARAGE GATE, KENSINGTON

*1 May 1920*

Here I come at last, darling Child mine, with one of my
longer scribbles!

First, as to the books sent this morning—four—all gifts.

(1) Herodotus—two volumes. The translation is excellent, and the notes very good. You must get to love, love

---

[3] French: Through the path of affliction
We arrive at the door of joy.

that genial creature—a sort of prose Greek Chaucer, a man with a genius for telling a story, and with a deep sense of religion too. You will find Book II (Egypt) quite delightful, most interesting. Why not do *that* most thoroughly, with Olivia? hitching it on to the Egyptian history learnt at school?

It is, however, a grave error to treat Herodotus as a genial old crony—where he describes countries and customs seen by himself, and events lived through by himself, he is *most* accurate, most reliable—e.g. Egypt and the Græco-Persian War.

(2) *British Museum Guide to the Egyptian Collection.* One of Dr. Wallis Budge's admirable books. Every word is worth considering, with the pictures as companion to Herodotus, Book II.

(3) Thucydides (mind that *y*, please!), *The Sicilian Expedition.* This is perhaps the finest, certainly the most rounded-off thing of Thucydides. Mind you study it most carefully—twice every word at least! The maps at the end, your occasional atlas, the *Little Classical Antiquities*—the coin book. All would help to make it all live and real—the only way to study histories.

(4) Thucydides—the *Speeches* in Jowett's translation. I should have liked to give you a complete translation. But the complete Jowett costs too much for just now. Besides it will be better if you first master the Sicilian Expedition part and these glorious speeches. Later on we can tackle the whole from cover to cover.

Of course, in the Thucydides *Speeches* you will look out technical terms in your *Antiquities*, and before tackling either Herodotus or Thucydides you will read up carefully what Gilbert Murray says about them in his *Greek Literature.*

Next as to Oxford. I was there three days. I had much the biggest audience I have ever had—till this I had 250 at most, this must have been some eight or nine hundred.

They were very attentive. I suppose four-fifths undergrad-
uates. Richard only three benches off, smiling and most
keen all the time; I felt it was a great support to see a
good many senior faces there which I knew well. But, besides, I always remember, on such occasions, what Socrates said so sensibly to his disciples preparing for public
speaking, that even the biggest audience is, after all, only
composed of individuals and of small groups, whom they
would have no fear at all to address. Also I find it important never to read, always to speak my things, to take care
to have humorous stories and not too great intervals; and
to manage little pauses, starting afresh in a different
voice. After the fifty-five-minutes-long address was over,
some two hundred and fifty people, almost all under-
graduates, came across to Queen's College Common
Room, and I had there, for an hour, to answer some ten
questions written down for me, from the spoken queries.
Only two or three were at all good, I thought; but still
such answerings do help to drive points into people's
heads. I felt it profoundly un-Protestant, but was pleased
to feel that its central point no thoughtful High Church
Anglican would deny. It *had* an edge, but not against Anglicanism—against Lutheranism; and yet I knew that at
least one keen Lutheran was listening, hoping, I am sure,
that I would turn out too superfine for the kind of stuff,
my Gwen, which I had to speak—if I would be truthful at
all.

My last two hours were spent with Richard—who did
the honours of his pretty little sitting-room very zealously.
He went and bought for the tea a fine chocolate cake.

He looked such a fine, large, clean, straight lad, as he
swung along the road by my side, without coat, hat or
umbrella—in spite of showers—and only his gown rolled
up round his neck and shoulders. I was a bit surprised to
hear a "No" to all my games questions—cricket, foot-
ball—

## Baron Friedrich von Hügel

I get the impression of a considerable dash of your father—of his simplicity and impulsiveness—and of a
streak of the Irishman, which, of course, he gets from his
other side. A streak which tends to make him intolerant
and absolute about people—and which might lead to
breaches and conflicts. But the lad is clean and sound,
and loves his mother dearly.

This time at Oxford has once more most vividly impressed me with the extraordinary greater happiness of
the adult or even of the latter life—soul: the soul's life is,
or at least can be, *then* so out of all proportion fuller,
richer, steadier, deeper than any young thing can possibly
attain. But how pathetic this makes them! I told them in
my address that I did not believe humility was for young
people at all. They, necessarily, knew, had done, had experienced so little—that they could not yet know their
immense limitations and deficiencies. I do not say this of
Richard—because he seems to me a modest lad.

Loving,
Father-Uncle.

*4 May 1920*

Child of my Heart,

Have just had your pathetic little lines. I too am over-
whelmed with work. And your and my work is *just the
same*, if we learn to do it simply for God, simply as, here
and now, the one means of growing in love for Him. To-
day it is cooking, scrubbing; to-morrow it may be utterly
different: death itself will come in due time, but, before it,
still many a joy and many a training. We will gently practise a genial concentration upon just the one thing picked
out for us by God. *How* this helps! *How* greatly we add to
our crosses by being cross with them! More than half our
life goes in weeping for things other than those sent us. Yet
it is these things, as sent, and when willed and at last

loved as sent, that train us for Home, that can form a spiritual Home for us even here and now.

The *Fioretti's* chapters are each complete in itself. Five minutes would give you rich food. And didn't St. Francis know such troubles as yours—bigger than yours, and didn't he just rise to them in all transforming love!

Of course, Child, I love you, as much, I do believe, as though I were your bodily father—it is as though that Great heart, your Father in God's other true world, had been allowed, and had loved, to touch my heart for you.

To-morrow I am sixty-eight, yet, thank God, I feel fresh and young in soul.

*From letter of 23 June 1920*

Child of my old Heart,

...

The wise way to fight antipathies is never to fight them directly—turn gently to other sights, images, thoughts, etc. If it—the hate—persists, bear it gently like a fever or a toothache—do not speak to it—better not speak of it even to God. But gently turn to Him your love and life, and tell Him gently that you want Him and all of Him: and that you beg for courage whilst He thus leaves you dressed, or seeing yourself dressed, in what you do not want to endorse as a will decision, but only as purgation if so He wills. It is an itch—scratching makes it worse. Away out into God's great world—even if your immediate landscape is just your unlovely antipathies.

Pray for your Uncle to become very, very humble—to disappear from one's own sight—with just God and souls; and one's little self one of these souls; how glorious that would be.

Delighted you love St. C.: *how* real she was!

Loving old Uncle,

H.

*Baron Friedrich von Hügel*

COURTFIELD, ROSS, HEREFORDSHIRE

*10 August 1920*

Darling Gwen-Child,

I want, though a bit late, to go over with you the points—the nooks and corners—of your Odstock environment and life. ... And I want to finish up by a good story or two and some facts, that may awaken and amuse still further your anyhow lively three.

As to Odstock, I greatly loved seeing, actually living for a day with you, in that precise concrete time and space condition in and through which my child has to grow into Eternity and God—the Ever Abiding. I so much cared for the Old Yew Inn, and the genial old owner, who made himself very pleasant to me as he drove me down towards the ever-graceful spire of the cathedral, with his old, rather weary, white pony. An excellent thing, having such a man and such a conveyance for yourself and the children.

...

Then I loved your room and, during that hour or more I was there, I felt it was peopled with the crowds of wholesome, peaceful apprehensions of the Gwen-child. How it was here especially that Christ and God helped and would help to turn isolation or crowdedness, natural overvehemence, pain, perplexity, pleasure and joy—all—all into gold, into love of God and gradual assimilation to Himself. I was especially glad to see that Crucifix there. Let people say what they will, there never existed, there will never exist, a symbol so deep, so comprehensive, so realist and yet so ideal, of our august religion—as just simply the Crucifix. I once read an address by the late Dean Stanley, in which that brilliant superficiality denounced the Crucifix as a mediaeval skull-and-crossbones grotesqueness, and contrasted this morbid extravagance with the poetry and smiling restraint of the Catacombs and *their* symbols—Christ as Orpheus, Christ as Good Shepherd, etc. As if the admitted absence of the Crucifix there did not spring from two very certain causes only— the fear of giving the Pagans any clear clue as to which is meant for Christ (lest such acutely hostile Pagans should thereupon deface or otherwise dishonour the image); and, again, the fear lest those early, not yet traditionally rooted Roman Christians, should have their faith strained rather than strengthened by the presentation of God hanging on the (Roman) gallows—gallows these (the Cross) which were employed only upon slaves—runaway or the like *ca-naille.*

And lastly, child, I so loved your little dim pre-Reformation church—so quiet and so devotional, so placed as though made specially for Gwen. There you can so well practise your institutionalism, your Holy Communions; but also your special Recollections, your Prayer of Quiet, and your praying for us all. How I shall love it, if any keen trouble or deep joy coming to you, you can and do run thither, whilst it all is thus keen, to give it to, to share it with—God—Christ! It is in that precise environment, by means of those aids that you, Blessing, can and will become deep and darling, humble and holy. There is simply *no* obstacle, given God's grace and a good will, and for these we will try and make our whole lives a prayer. Loving old Father-Uncle,

F. v. Hügel.

13 VICARAGE GATE

*From letter of 31 August 1920*

My own darling Gwen,

Here I have a fine lot of things to talk to you about. Two from you and three from myself ....

I am struck too at how the little regarded, the very simple, unbrilliant souls—souls treated by impatient others as more or less wanting, are exactly pretty often specially enlightened by God and specially near to Him. And there, no doubt, is the secret of this striking interconnection between an apparent minimum of earthly gifts and a maximum of heavenly light. The cause is not that gifts of quick-wittedness, etc., are bad, or are directly obstacles to Grace. No, no. But that quite ordinary intelligence—real slowness of mind—will quite well do as reflections of God's light, and that such limitations are more easily accompanied by simplicity, naïveness, recollection, absence of self-occupation, gratefulness, etc., which dispositions are necessary for the soul's union with God. Such souls more easily approach action—and more easily escape activity.

...

A wonderful thoughtful friend insisted to me that the soul's health and happiness depended upon a maximum of *zest* and as little as possible of excitement. *Zest* is the pleasure which comes from thoughts, occupation, etc., that fit into, that are continuous, applications, etc., of extant habits and interests of a good kind—duties and joys that steady us and give us balance and centrality. *Excitement* is the pleasure which comes from breaking loose, from fragmentariness, from losing our balance and centrality. Zest is natural warmth—excitement is fever heat. For zest—to be relished—requires much self-discipline and recollection—much spaciousness of mind: whereas the more distracted we are, the more racketed and impulse-led, the more we thirst for excitement and the more its sirocco air dries up our spiritual sap and makes us long for more excitement ....

And that "side-shows"—*queer* things religiously—that what is not central, sober, balanced, may indeed still help certain souls in certain ways; but that, for ourselves, we should carefully eschew being drawn into attending to them, and thus weakening our *own* centrality.

But my Gwen-child will feed upon zest—and zest-bringing things, she will more and more become so central that even if she lives thirty years more than this old scribbler, she will be able with little or no human encouragement to escape excitement, lopsidedness, oddity, etc. ....

I write perhaps too emphatically because I am just now suffering over a very bad *lurch* of a woman I know well—a strange bit of sheer thirst for change at any price; of the weakness I have learnt sorrowfully to be prepared suddenly to come up against, in almost any woman.

My own first point brings up once more a matter we have often considered, but which I do not think we can ever get too much cleared up. A friend of mine, whom I have known for forty-five years, died some days back, at seventy-six without any traceable shred of religion (at least in the ordinary sense of the word). He was a man of finely clean life, full of philanthropy, genuine and costly, a cultivated man, a scholar, also a man of naturally religious temper. It is certainly impossible to know the depths of any soul: yet certain points are once more clear to me, over this further case—that the agnostic tempest which roared between say 1855 and 1875 was so violent, that no wonder quick-witted lads went under, many, many of them. That even so, the finer ones managed to retain much that was high and right—even that was touchingly Christian—but that they owed this, not to Agnosticism, but to the Christian faith, the tradition from which they had broken away less than they themselves thought. And finally that, not only did they show faults or limitations—who does not?—but that these limitations were readily traceable to their Agnosticism. (I could easily draw out the details of this in my friend.)

...

A matter of great delight to me just now is *a charming, most gentlemanly* and cultivated young Japanese, who speaks French and capital English, and who reads difficult German books with ease—a definite, indeed fervent, Christian—a Roman Catholic, who is finishing his training for a Japanese Government (University) Professorship of Philosophy. I am having a long talk with him once a week. He mourns to me over the intense materialism of his race and country, and evidently feels keenly the need for the whole poor modern world (aped by the Japs) to return to its senses—to God and the spiritual life as the true end of man. He wants to be helped find the best means of commending Christianity to such, at bottom, thorough Easterns. But I want to concentrate rather upon getting him to feel and to pursue still more precisely and vividly than he does, the special genius, the driving force of Christianity. I feel him that very, very rare combination—much intellect and still more soul! Pray for him, and for the Loving old,

Fatherly Thing.

13 VICARAGE GATE, W. 8

*4 October, St. Francis's Day, 1920*

My ever darling Gwen-Child,

Here I am, at last, once more scribbling to you! I have really not missed a single day on which I *could* have done so. First, there was the getting ready for Oxford—a big business, because one of us four paper givers delayed everything by his absence abroad; then returned to England to say that *now* (some changes having occurred while news could not reach him) he could not, and would not, join in; then let another man write a paper in his stead; and then—when this poet thing had actually printed his hurried contribution, paff! came back into the game and gave us a (fifth) paper after all! Then last week was very full with Oxford—our five little speeches, each one about his own paper, and as to what he agreed and disagreed with in the other four papers—this on Sunday, 26 September, with Mr. Balfour in the chair and speaking also, when we five had spoken. *I* made the first little speech, but spoke, I was told, too fast and too shortly. Then came a French professor, a good friend of mine, a fervent Roman Catholic. The little speech was excellent in its substance, but, it was generally thought, too mathematically demonstrative in method and tone. Then followed Professor S— —, the man who had led us such a life—able but very unsatisfactory—has, somehow, quite lost the sense of what religion is, and of why we so greatly need religion. Then came Principal Jacks, head of the Unitarian College in Oxford, who, on our subject, "The Relation between Morals and Religion," had distressed me, by printing in his paper that a belief in a Beloved Community (=a Church without God) was quite equivalent, as a motive for morality, to faith in God. In his speech Dr. Jacks was chiefly busy with that very vague, Pantheistic thinker, Professor Wildon Carr, and thus busy in a smart journalistic sort of way. And finally came this Professor Wildon Carr—very thin, very abstract, a good bit hurt with Dr. Jacks.—Mr. Balfour's speech was beautiful. All morality, in the precise degree of its depth and truth, consists in a continuous and an increasing sacrifice of lower motives for higher and ever higher motives. Yet we cannot, we do not, make such great searching sacrifices for nothing, into the blue. We make them, we *can* make them, only for reality; and the highest motive, love, demands and finds that Reality to be the highest possible Reality, love, God. Hurrah!

It had been planned that then objections would be raised to these six speeches; and that each of the six speakers would have ten minutes for reply. But nothing of this came about. For two Frenchmen now managed to break in—the one to explain and defend the nonreligious moral teaching in the French State school; the other to try and show that, at all times, the French State schools had taught a Positivism. Especially this last, a tiny little man, was interminable, and quietly continued his exposition *twice* after Mr. Balfour had pulled him up for being beyond the time allotted to us all. This meeting lasted three hours. Then on Monday and Tuesday I saw many friends and new acquaintances, mostly connected with the Congress. And then on Tuesday evening my great friend, Professor Kemp Smith of Edinburgh, came home here with me for two nights. The two full days of his stay required all my strength for my talks with him—a large, religious soul as well as a highly-trained intellect.

He said a number of striking things. That the age of the largest spiritual mortality amongst men was in middle life. That he had first been struck with this when a great gathering of all its past and present students took place at Princeton University, U.S.A. You had to pass over the young men, some of whom, indeed, looked unsettled, uncertain, but not lost to faith and heroism, and to move on to the men in their forties: and, alas, how many self-centred, dried-up, all-to-pieces, cynical countenances!—Then what piercing insight into souls he has got! He talked of a cultivated, clean-lived ex-Roman Catholic priest whom I also know, and whom the average man would, I think, never feel to be anything but all right: "Why, the man is all to pieces: the wish-wash of the newspapers—progress, etc.—is all he knows or believes. All true insight is gone."—Then, too, this: "More and more I am coming to see that the chief source of errors is subjectivism, is distrust of, disbelief in, the natural, normal intimations of our senses, of our reason, of our conscience, of our religious sense."—And when I told him (brought up a Presbyterian) of how one of the members of our "Religion" Society had recently asked to be allowed to appear as a "D"—"Detached," because he had ceased to find any use whatsoever, for himself, in churches, sacraments, etc.: he, Kemp Smith, shivered as though pierced by a sharp instrument.

My Gwen: my doings have cost me a good deal: I know why. The fact is that like all three of my daughters, I have a very vehement, violent, over-impressionable nature, which, on such occasions, gets ridiculously over-roused, jarred, confused. Hence I have then a big job (quite apart from all visible doings) to drop, drop, drop all this fever-ishness, and to listen, as docilely as I can, to think, will and pray, with only "la fine pointe de l'esprit,"[4] as St. François de Sales and Fénelon never weary in recom-mending. I tell you this, Child, because I am sure you are much like that yourself, and hence may encourage you along the same path of a most necessary stillness and peace. The minute I at all attain to these dispositions, fruitfulness succeeds to fever. So with Gwen!

I have been thinking about and praying much to-day for an American lady in far-away Chicago who has been both comforting and alarming me by her entirely unsolic-ited communications—three in number—that she is the now fifty-three-years-old wife of a university professor—a man of nobly clean life and spiritual mind, but no definite religious belief whatsoever—and mother to four children, of twenty-three, seventeen, fourteen and seven; that till some two years ago she herself was an Agnostic; that then, more and more, St. Catherine of Genoa, in my *Mysti-cal Elements*, seized hold of her, and the instinct that she might still come to believe much, if only she attained to much humility and to much love of God's poor; and, now, that she had fairly made up her mind to submit to Rome to-day, on St. Francis's Day, she a Frances.—Her very Protestant, touching mother-in-law was in this my room with me, a week or so ago, to speak her mind and to draw out my own.—Both to the daughter-in-law in Chicago and to the mother-in-law in London I said: that neither in that

---

[4] French: "the fine point of the spirit"

book nor in my life did I, or do I aim at making Roman
Catholics: that would be odious presumption. That God
and His grace are (in various degrees, no doubt) everywhere—but specially, very especially, in Christianity. That
the presumption is always in favour of souls remaining,
as to institutional appurtenance, where they are—it being
God's affair to make it clear to them if, doing their best
where they are, He wants them elsewhere. That no æs-
thetic, etc., attraction, no preference are enough: that only
the sense of obligation in and for the particular soul
should decide.—The dear old lady was very touching, but
I saw quickly that even the bare possibility that her
daughter-in-law could be seeking anything but services
more gorgeous than were those of the Ritualists, etc., did
not, doubtless could not, enter her head. So then I told her
I had a darling Niece who had found God and Christ and
Church—oh, so really; and that I loved to help her all I
could without a thought of her moving. That I would
gladly help, if I could, in a similar way, with her daughter-in-law. Still, that we really cannot, can we? become
other people's conscience. The dear old thing thereupon
seemed satisfied with my declaring that I well understood
how *very* much she disliked Rome; how sad and hurt she
was, etc.—To the daughter-in-law I wrote that my Niece
had an Anglican clerical adviser of a deeply Catholic
mind, and more spiritual assuredly than any but the finest (the rare) Roman Catholic trainers. And that's true, my
Gwen. Loving old Uncle,
 H.

13 VICARAGE GATE, KENSINGTON

*26 October 1920*

My ever darling Child,
 Again late, but again not in fault as to this lateness—
brain gets feverish as soon as ever I add even such a scrib-

ble as this to any considerable work—and my work, or rather my jobs, have been considerable since I last wrote. But I loved getting your second letter; and you must never, please, await an answer from me, if you have something further to say, and find the time to say it in.

I am delighted you are about to get this, your first real Retreat; and I do not doubt that you will be greatly refreshed and braced by it.—No doubt, a Retreat depends *somewhat* upon the Giver of it; yet it really depends far more upon the simplicity and generosity of the soul that makes the Retreat. I am sure you already know well that you must evade all straining, all vehemence, all, as it were, putting your nerves into it. On the contrary the attention wanted is a leisurely expansive one—a dropping gently of all distractions, of obsessions, etc. "La fine pointe de l'esprit," that is the instrument of progress, the recipient of Graces. This old scribbler—how much of that dropping, evading, gently waiting—as against his interior vehemences and uproar, a sterile and sterilising restlessness—he has to practise! Yet the practice shows him plainly (in the long run) that *that* is what good sense and God want of him: peace and power come *that* way and only that way.

I know too that you well understand that you should never strain—never directly strive—to like people. Just merely drop or ignore your antipathies. There, again, I have been having hurricanes of antipathies—well, to keep quietly ignoring all that rumpus—that is all that God asks. And we then grow, through, and on occasion of, these involuntary vehemences—they keep us humble and watchful and close to God. I would suggest, too, especially for the Retreat time, not to make too many or too complicated resolutions; or rather, on the last day, to cut down the number of these reached by, say, a half. The remainder will probably be as much as you can wisely attend to *out of Retreat*, till next retirement.

## Baron Friedrich von Hügel

The American lady is to reach London on Saturday night—30 October, and she leaves for America on 13 November. She writes from Paris and says she is much looking forward to talks with me. She is evidently a very genuine and sincere, but also a very unusual woman. She writes that she has no attraction either to God or to Christ—that in these directions she is perplexed; but that the one thing that draws and feeds her is the Church—the assembly of believers throughout the world. In Paris she spends as much time as possible in the churches, amidst the worshippers—that this somehow infects her with faith. She has all her life (fifty-three years old now) been an Agnostic; but this, somehow, breaks that spell! I tell her that very certainly the Church is for Christ and God, and not vice versa—very certainly. Yet that, after all, she loves the Church because it infects her with belief. Hence, she wants to believe, and delights in belief when it comes, and the belief is evidently not simply belief in the Church (is such a thing possible?), but belief in what the Church believes— in Christ, in God.

She did not take the move on 4 October that she thought she was likely to take. But evidently still *that* is in her mind. I shall, however, understand her case more definitely when I have seen her. I am proposing to her, our first meeting should be on All Saints' at early Mass, with a talk after breakfast.

My sweet, of course *you* will be most welcome here on 5 November. We can, I hope, have a good talk afterwards.

I am so glad you begin your Retreat on All Saints'—my favourite Feast—the Feast not only of all the heroic lovers of God that have ever lived, but the Feast of single, heroic, supernatural acts, even if and where they remained single. May that darling glow, that genial sunshine of the saints, with Christ their King in their midst, deepen, widen, sweeten, expand, steady this darling little child! And pray for us all, Dearie!

Of course a second weekly Holy Communion would be excellent; but this must not be forced. God will provide reasonable easy means, if *that* is His will.

Loving old Uncle,

F. v. Hügel

13 VICARAGE GATE, KENSINGTON, W. 8

*23 November 1920*

My darling Child,

I loved your letter of 15 November very much. And now I must really try to answer its points, where these invite an answer, and to tell you the chief things that I have been learning from various happenings since my last.

1. I feel with you that a very big question is that whether or not to keep up your violin. Indeed, next to your elementary religious practices and attending to the children, I can find none as big. I am only sorry that it should have to be a question at all—you know well how I deliberately put your non-religious readings *after* the fiddling. I could not give you a bigger proof of the importance I attach to that violining; for as you know, I believe much in the utility, *also and especially for one's religion,* of such an alternation of non-religious study. I have often explained this to you; and my life witnesses to its truth to me every day.

A pity that the problem has always to be "two and a half hours a day of practice or none." For you could doubtless get in an hour or an hour and a half without any crush. Yet I quite understand that it really has to remain at that alternative.

Well, I only hope much that you will, somehow, be able to retain the fiddling—those two and a half hours, even if it means no non-religious reading and possibly also the abandonment of one or other regular occupation besides. I am sure your music is worth it already, from its effect upon your happiness. So I trust you will be given light, not to abandon it, but how, without any dereliction of any real duty, to keep it regularly in you life.

And if Richard really takes to music for life and for his livelihood: *there* is another, big reason for keeping up your music fully.

2. I am very glad you are again visiting the poor people—I am sure you have real gifts that way. I have always much regretted that my deafness has so crippled me in that direction. I feel as if it would have done me much good, even though I am not sure whether I would have had gifts that way.

3. As to the Fénelon, I am ever so glad that you love him so. But indeed I felt sure you would. But I kept him back till now because I always fear as to him just only one thing: that the reader may have too little experience of spiritual things to perceive, under all that apparent ease and suave simplicity, the masses of spiritual experience and of religious wisdom. But you by now have sufficient experience to bring to him, to perceive what lots and lots he brings to you.

Among the letters I feel that perhaps those which will suit you most and will teach you most are the letters to Sœur Charlotte de S. Cyprien. Oh, what a lot I owe to them; they are often, often gently ringing through my soul. The biographical "Notice" will have made you realise her as an ex-Huguenot—a woman of great mind and the toughest will, but naturally haughty, contemptuous of the average, requiring (as my Gwen-child does) to learn to lose herself in and for the average. If God, if Christ, loves men—and who can doubt it?—He loves *the average* very much—the poor little virtue, the poor little insight. How splendidly Fénelon feels in her a certain unchristian aristocraticalness of mind—she was evidently a sort of Dean Inge in petticoats. Mind, Sweet, you bathe in, you saturate yourself with, those letters!

Then there are those letters to the two dukes (Chevreuse and Beauvilliers): what grand direction as to how to lead a *very full* and yet a leisurely life! Do you notice there, St. Catherine's "one thing at a time"? And here there is also the insistence upon doing this one thing always with a certain environment of peace, of non-hurry around it. I find this double practice of golden worth; and, in getting up of a morning, I gently plan the day's doings, not too many of them for the application to them of Fénelon's treatment. (One has, of course, to be ready to modify one's scheme, as sudden, unexpected duties crop up in the day. But, even so, that gentle scheme is useful.)

Do you notice one very wonderful thing in Fénelon? It is the combination of a rarely light (not frivolous)—a light and elastic open temperament with an earnest will and gently concentrated determination. People as determined and as ardent as he, usually are, or become, heavy, rigoristic. And again, people as light and elastic as he, usually are, or become, frivolous and corrupt. By that combination—the earnestness without rigorism—he always strikes me as belonging, in his measure, to that minority of Christian teachers who have reached closest to that same combination in Our Lord Himself—to have caught up a few drops of that genial rain, that royally generous west wind, that gently drops and brightly blows through the virile sunshine of His love. St. Francis is another, and, of course, a much greater instance of that delightful paradox. The future of religion, indeed even already its present propagation in our poor old world, lie in it.

4. You are doubtless unable to keep on with the Herodotus, *that* may be able to come some time later. Oh, I love him much: he is so childlike, so quaint, so wholesome, a little like a Greek prose Chaucer, I think. And then his general tone is so truly religious; what a dread he has of all arrogance, and of its blinding effects and inevitable terrible falls!

5. As to Mrs. — —, she went off to America on Saturday, 13 November. We had four long talks, besides meeting twice in church. I think she will really persevere and will greatly grow, for she is deeply humble and very anxious to become still more so, and possesses a remarkable self knowledge — knows how to distinguish what in herself is a surface mood and what is underlying, often very different genuine substance. So on the evening of her first Holy Communion day, she said, with a mischievous smile: "I trust and believe I shall never lose this my new, fuller light: you see, I do not think I have ever felt so Protestant as I have done to-day!" But I wish (it is only a peripheral matter) that she did not put her political radicalism so high in her scheme of things.

13 VICARAGE GATE, W. 8

*From letter of 8 December 1920*

My darling Gwen-Child,
I have to thank you for three very dear good letters — as always very welcome and very carefully read. I think the following points are those I see clear about, or as to which I have facts worth reporting about.

1. *As to Fénelon.* I am delighted you love him so. He is one of the, say, half-dozen of the non-Scriptural writers who has helped me most directly and most copiously in my own interior life — a life requiring *immensely* that daily, hourly, death to self I believe that less keen and violent natures *can* get harm from him; phlegmatic, drifting, inert temperaments could take him wrong way on. But I doubt whether he himself, the living man, ever harmed any soul he tried to help, and he was too amazingly penetrative of the particular soul before him thus to harm. The only possible exception is, *I think*, his cousin, Madame Guyon: possibly by his disciple attitude towards her, he did, as a matter of fact, help her to become still more the *Quietist*

than she would have been without him. Certainly it was for the purpose of covering her exceedingly vague and wool-gathering expressions that in his *Explications des Maximes des Saints* he strained his own language, and got censured by Rome for such terms. But then I have never taken him in that *livre manqué,* but in these letters; and again in these letters, as a man of immense action and persevering, energising of will, addressing souls too vehement and too intense, taken like this I have found him tremendously helpful. Do not hurry to return these four volumes ....

I am sending you three other volumes of the Correspondence — the letters to his family and the mixed letters. This because I have found that his helpfulness was greatly increased by my realising him as a thoroughly flesh and blood, naturally faultful individual, and as a man to whom God was not sparing of much, *much* trial and purification. ... They do, you will find, humanise, concretise one's image of him greatly, and here and there appears a letter, perhaps as many as a dozen all told, which really *are* spiritual letters. — Also pray specially notice and read and re-read M. Tronson's letters: that good soul, the trainer of Fénelon at S. Sulpice. Pray note Tronson's austerity and *immense* ideal for Fénelon, and his piercing analysis of his natural faults. A fine example of what I so want my Child to grasp vividly, and for good and all, that *usually* one thoroughly trained spiritual soul has in the background another trained spiritual soul as its trainer.

2. *As to Du Bose.* I want you, Dearie, first of all to realise that Du Bose is not — up to this his swan's song — one of my men at all. His books are treated as gospels by many young High Anglican clerics. But they deeply dissatisfy me. Three ideas are with him throughout; and I am very confident that all three are gravely mistaken and highly impoverishing.

(i.) God and man are in the whole work of sanctification, salvation, etc., on a *strict parity*. God's action never extends farther than man's action. They are not only *both* wanted in some degree: right! But they are both, in actual fact, always and necessarily equal in depth and in breadth. What stuff, what blasphemy!

(ii.) The possibility of Sin is a necessary part of Liberty as such. In sheer thought, in the very nature of things, to be free to do and be good, is to be free and do the reverse — evil. No — and again *no*. To be able to do, to be evil, is a defect, a restriction on liberty. Perfect liberty always spontaneously, joyously wills its own perfect nature. We should feel humbled, not only by our actual sins, but already by the fact that we can commit such things. (This alone cuts the ground from under all the Byronisms as childish unreason.)

(iii.) There is an element of potential evil in God Himself. (This follows, of course, inevitably from No. ii.) No and again No. You know how I try to account for the existence of evil in the world, but even if I were wrong in my particular solution for the existence of evil — Du Bose's should be fought to the death.

Du Bose has still further notions hardly more sound than these. But these are surely enough. You will see then that, not as a further specimen of a teaching I believe in, but, on the contrary, as a *first* pathetically late instance of a *sound* spiritual yearning in contrast with painfully reckless or at least inadequate theorisings, I have loved the strain (the strain more than the actual words) of this paper, in so far as it hungers for the Church.

By the way, the sad unsatisfactoriness of Du Bose's own all but life-long subjectivist Protestantism, helps me to see how little ideal is that abounding in its own sense of each of the sound currents of Protestantism which Du Bose even in this paper tries to make out to be somehow really satisfactory. In reality *each soul* requires centrality, inclusiveness, balance, sobriety, immense reverence. Its errors may get counterbalanced in the course of history and for mankind at large by the contrary errors, or its incompleteness may be made up for by the contrary incompletenesses of other souls. Well—but what about this soul itself? As to the particular sentence you quote as to the *Church as the only Christ* in which we are and we can do anything by Him and for Him—I think you have spotted a seriously excessive phrase. The Church is not Christ—is no more Christ than it is God. We require God and Christ and Church: each in and with the other. But it ruins the whole richness, indeed the truth, of the outlook, if any one of these—especially if the Church is simply identified with either of the other two. But there you have just a small touch of Du Bose's weakness, which in his books runs riot—he overstates till he meets, implies, the very opposite of what he started out to defend.

(3) *As to your own Church appurtenance.* I want to say very simply and definitely what I have long felt with you, Child, but what I have, perhaps, rather implied than at any time expressed *en toute lettre*—that I find God in His goodness has given you a very—a sensitively Catholic mind; that I never think of you, feel you as a Protestant at all, but as an elementary, inchoate, deep Catholic soul. I think you really seize upon and feed upon those doctrines and practices in Anglicanism which, thank God, are Catholic, and there's an end on't—and that you instinctively shrink from what may be un-Catholic or even anti-Catholic there, especially in the vigorous kite-flying which some junior Anglicans somehow love to practise. The latter part of the sentence means that I believe traditional High Anglicanism—the stock that Edward Talbot springs from, contains really but little that is not Catholic. It is not complete, but it is, in its positive teaching, upon the whole, most consolingly Catholic.

## Baron Friedrich von Hügel

Now I must admit that when I began trying to help you spiritually, I felt it might be my duty, or at least the wiser course, to give you, and encourage you in, not Roman Catholic books, but Anglican ones. This might help to keep you from thinking of Rome. — But then I saw, on careful examination, that I had no even indirect intention to woo you for Rome, through your spiritual reading. I simply wanted to give you the best, the strongest, food for your soul. Was I really to eschew what I believe to be best, simply because it *might* indirectly awaken comparisons, misgivings, etc.? As a point of detail I had thought of starting you on Newman's *Parochial and Plain Sermons* — certainly classics and well known to me. But then these sermons are rigorist — how they have depressed me! Just the opposite from Fénelon, who always braces me. And really, I cannot allow you to be depressed — at least I cannot organise depression for you! — But William Law, and recently Dean Church, have written spiritual things that are not depressing, and that, some time you might read with profit. — However, High Anglicans themselves live largely upon the books I have recommended to you. Indeed, I know some such who would be indignant with me for not considering these books as somehow really Anglican. — After all, you can and will just feed on what truly helps you there to love God and Christ, and to hate, and constantly to guard against self. All this will fit in beautifully with your praying in the little church — your Holy Communion there and in the cathedral. I think your thoughts at times about Rome as possibly for yourself probably *are* a good deal a wish to be at one with your old uncle. But I have already explained how truly I feel ourselves at one. And short of a very clear light that you *must* join, that it would be sin not to, you might easily cross over and find yourself *less* at one with me than now. Now you are getting the finest Church teachings and figures in these books — and the weaknesses, the humannesses of

Anglicans furnish a foil. Then you would be environed by
the poor *average*, with *its* weaknesses and humannesses —
very real there also. — Hence I would have you, my Sweet,
do your very best where you are, with what you there can
get; taking care only not to fix yourself up negatively — I
mean against Roman Catholicism. Consider it simply as
what, even if the fuller truth, does not concern you now —
perhaps never will. After all it is a truth which, in large
part, you are living already, and which you can and will
live more and more, without any shutting up of yourself.

Loving old Uncle-Father,

F.v.H.

I was so sorry about the headache, but glad about the
peace. Death and Peace — Good!

But indeed, above all, it will be your love of them in
and for Christ — your love of and union with Him, which
will keep or gain them for God. After all, every soul, boy
or girl, as they grow up, have to pass through that delicate difficult crisis, when they themselves have deliberately to will the right and God. Even when the training and
example have been perfect, and when the natural character is specially good. And, *of course*, it is your call to work
for, and be ready, and be by, those three and their father
also. From prayer and solitude back to them, and from
them again back to it: and with them much in your prayer
and your prayer much in them — *there* is a fine rich tension
for you. Bless you, Child, for 1921.

Loving old,

Fatherly One.

13 VICARAGE GATE, KENSINGTON, W. 8

*29 January-2 February 1921*

My darling Gwen-Child,

I think of you as back at Odstock, and, in any case, ready for a letter. I have had to be a bit long before getting to this one, but have not a bit forgotten you, Dear. There are three things or four that I specially want to write about this time.

1. Your music. I still await light on this point. For, on the one hand, it does look as if the necessary amount of violin practice were straining to the head; yet, on the other hand, this music-producing is such a unique vehicle of self-expression for you. I should be so loath to see you give it up. The *crux* of the difficulty lies evidently in the *amount* — the *large* amount of practice necessary for your otherwise stiff fingers. If, say, an hour or an hour and a half a day were sufficient — that would not seriously strain the head. But then you seem to be sure that *that* would not be enough! I do not feel that the possible impossibility of keeping up that full orchestra for performances in the cathedral need decide the matter. For though it is, of course, specially inspiring to play thus in God's house — indeed in one of the old cathedrals — yet it would not, surely, be impossible this failing — for your organist friend to get up chamber-concerts, quartets, in which you would be first (sole first) violin — concerts which, of course, could be for some solid charity, and which could be spiritually intentioned by my Gwen-child.

2. A couple of attempts to help souls seem to have gone awry with me just now: I mention the cases because you too will, sooner or later, doubtless yourself have more or less similar experiences. One was of an Italian man friend of about forty-five — an immense reader and somewhat intemperately speculative mind — a man who came back to Christianity, indeed to the Roman Catholic

Church, from wildly secularist Socialism some eight years ago. I had built great hopes of rare help for him from a Jesuit Retreat which I suggested his making for now about a year. At last he went and made one, the other day. But the priest who gave him the Retreat, an American, though a very good man, rather turned it into a series of theological speculations or discussions than that he kept it, and made it, into directly practical instructions in prayer, meditation, training of the conscience, discovery and reformation of personal faults, etc.—which is, of course, the direct object and function of a Retreat. I do not think those four full days have damaged my man, but they fed just his speculative bent, which I hoped would be starved, and have starved his devotional needs and chances which I hoped would be fed. Ah, well—God may be offering him chances I do not see or know of. He is a well-intentioned man, and God will bless even unlikely-looking happenings.

Then there is a young English lady artist, who adored her mother, who had no religion, or who had lost what she had had. This damsel came to stay for three nights a few days ago, and to our surprised pleasure seemed definitely religious in her outlook (a thing which had appeared to us to be sadly lacking in her). And she wrote me so enthusiastic a letter about my *Christianity and the Supernatural*—especially as to my tact with young people—that I thought I could and ought to say something about religion to her, so I wrote her a careful answer dwelling on the importance of cultivating this her religious sense, just as she cultivated her artistic sense; on the great Jewish-Christian-Mohammedan tradition of prayer for the dead, which she might get into the habit of for her mother; and on the great importance of whenever reasonably possible, only *preliminary* judgments. This last point because I had tried to introduce her to Browning's poetry—entirely unknown to her till I read aloud to her some six of his noblest easier pieces; and had found that she judged straight away and finally and with an angry hostility. As I pointed out, she could not, at that stage, know more than that, so far, she did not like him—after all, a very small fact, and one that might well be overcome on further acquaintance with writings which seniors of hers, well qualified to judge, had come to reckon of the rarest depth and richest delight. But this letter was answered by a curt, dry little note, telling me she had done all the things I proposed, now during several years. I was glad in a way, for surely even without any self-knowledge she must know whether or not she has gone to Holy Communion, often, indeed if possible every Sunday, and whether she has done at least fifteen minutes' spiritual reading every day. But then it was strange to note that she said "all the things," whilst it is clear that the suspense-of-any-avoidable-final-judgment practice had certainly not been done for several years. Ah, well; it does not follow that that letter was no use at all; and, in any case, one did one's little best.

3. Three dear friends have died since I last wrote—two of them quite old: fine old Dr. Alexander Whyte, the Presbyterian Edinburgh preacher and writer, a man with much of the Catholic mind in surroundings which made its utterance difficult; and fine old Lady Stawell (pronounced Stowell), the widow of an Australian official, a sweet, strong serene Anglican, a devoted Christian. She had many a trouble; but her heroic resignation to God's holy Will, her generous and strongly gentle application of her faith to her entire life and dispositions never left her to the last; and when I saw her lying dead on Sunday the countenance was indeed beautiful in its triumphant spirituality. These two friends were respectively in their middle eighties and late nineties. But the third friend was only fifty; and *he* was carried off instantaneously by angina pectoris. He was a very devoted, very popular, immensely active Jesuit priest—the man who gave me hospitality in the Jes-

uit house of studies these last four years at Oxford. He
was essentially a man of action, full of social service work.
Well, *that is* necessary too—necessary that some, with the
gift for it, should labour much at it. His devoted bulldog
Jimmy is sure to feel his master's death deeply: they were
inseparables, day and night.

13 VICARAGE GATE

*5 February 1921*

I think five to seven on the fourteenth will be best for
me—have me freshest for you. And Aunt Mary will love
to have you to tea at four-thirty. I would have mine alone
at that time, and we could thus start at five, having satisfied our lower wants.

But this is specially to wish you a very deep and devoted, a very peaceful and *épanoui*[5] birthday. What shall I
wish you specially for the coming year—for all the years
of your life? I will wish you the ever increasing practice of
just the kind of moderation, alternation, mixedness, which
you are already seeing and practising. It is the moderation
of yourself in all things—especially also in your religion—
and in your very prayer; your always occupying a very
appreciable part of your clock-time and direct attention
with not-directly religious things; and this precisely because of, and for, God; to ensure stability, sobriety, genuine detachment also, especially, in the deepest things and
joys. This practise and organise, this make instinctive: and
you will persevere to the end, you will grow more and
more spiritual and holy; you will gain solid joy: you will
become utterly true and elastic and accessible. Even at
seventy, in such a life, "vainly the flesh fades, soul makes
all things new."

---

[5] French: "open" (as a flower opens)

*Baron Friedrich von Hügel*

Holy Communion, for you, to-morrow.
Fatherly One,
H.

*8 February 1921*

I had intended, Child, not to write again before we meet on the fourteenth. But I had forgotten that already to-morrow is Ash Wednesday — Lent beginning! So I write this little card to say that we will both of us, will we not? make our Lenten penitence consist primarily in the ever gently renewed dropping of our several over-intense-nesses, and in as gently and really adaptably as we can, accepting, fitting into, the rubs and jolts, the disappointments and drearinesses which God in His merciful training of us may allow or send us. And we will both add to this central chief thing just one or two little renunciations. Am dropping my after-dinner fruit and all book-buying till Easter. You may be able to start some little thing like that to-morrow. And for the rest, the darling poor, the open air, the Greek books, the dear dog, and any duty that may come to hand; all penetrated by your Holy Communions and an expansive, humble joy.
Fatherly One.

13 VICARAGE GATE, KENSINGTON

*22 February 1921*

Ever darling Child Mine,
I got your last letter yesterday morning, and though it was (as far as you yourself, your dispositions and affections go) as dear as ever you are, it nevertheless — through no fault of yours, but through much stupidity of my own — gave me grave distress and uneasiness. You see, as I have told you many a time, the biggest cross of my little old life which God has deigned to train by not a few trials,

*103*

was when (all unintentionally, indeed for long quite un-
wittingly, but none the less really) I myself, so to speak,
*put out my True's spiritual eyes.* I myself, who had chiefly
trained her in faith and trust and love of God and Christ
and Church, so strained and perplexed that very sensitive
young soul that her very love of me and her natural openness to all impressions from me, bereft her for years of all
faith — or at least of all peace, of all conscious faith. As I
also told you, I had the *immense* consolation of seeing her
come back fully, even before she married, of seeing with
my own eyes in Rome, her darling, utterly, deeply spontaneously Christian and Catholic faith, love, life and death.
She knew well, of course, how little comfort I should gain
by any even of this, if there was in it anything to suggest
that it was done in an attempt to please me: if what is essentially a free, self-responsible act and donation was performed even from such a touching but quite inadequate
motive. Yet she knew, of course, what a unique joy it
would give me if I could see here on earth my miserable
blind work undone. And so, when she became just ill
enough to receive Extreme Unction, she turned to me so
darlingly, "Oh, Papa, what a grace, what a joy, to receive
a further Sacrament of the Church." I knew exactly why
she thus turned first to me. And then she pressed for, she
got permission, to receive this Sacrament again, and was,
the sweet, a little hurt that I did not seem to her as utterly
assured of her love in so receiving it, as she wanted me to
be, and as she knew I well could be. And so, of course,
also with her confession, and above all with Holy Communion: but with these the evidence of her full return to
the Catholic faith and practice had been before me for
some eight or nine years. Now, Sweet: since my True died,
I do not think I have cared to try and serve and feed any
soul as much as yours. My chief prayer has been that I
might never strain, never complicate, never perplex you,
and that in a Fénelon-like self oblivion I might just simply

help and feed and carry you, if and when and where you required it—to let God lead. Well, Sweet, up to this last interview I think (with doubtless many little imperfections) God mercifully helped me to do what I believe He wanted me to do. But I suppose I was getting to count on my poor little insight or other highly-limited capacities, and it was time I should have a wholesome humiliation. I feel sure that this is good for me. But may I not have done any permanent harm to you, Child mine! I mean: may I not have conveyed impressions so vivid that (however erroneously, they have so shaped and affected your mind) I cannot now seriously modify them? I will try, as surely is my clear duty, presently. But I want first to get three smaller points out of the way.

1. *As to health and music.* I am so sorry about the neuritis in the right arm, and the (of course inevitable) suspension of all violining. You will indeed be wise if you suspend or sufficiently moderate or modify whatever else may now tire or strain you. In this way you will soon get well again. And meanwhile you need not, need you? make any definite decisions as to the music. For I take it, that once in your average health again, you could manage an hour to an hour and a half a day without any marked physical disadvantage.

2. *As to your mother's questions.* It must be some twenty-five years ago that your mother once began to write me about some marriage matter—and asking some question, I forget what. I answered her as plainly as she had asked. And it tried me a good bit after, later on, when I found that she had told several of her friends about my answer—as very odd—as a sort of queer joke—yet, what a sweet woman she is—with such dear darling qualities! So, though I have, since then, been always reluctant to answer questions of hers, I wish her nothing but good, and would like to help her when and where I solidly can do so.

*Letters to a Niece*

(i.) *As to the Virgin Birth.* I always find most help myself by dwelling upon the very early, the contemporary conviction of our Lord's sinlessness—something quite different and distinct from all and every other human holiness: and upon the consequent early feeling and belief that One thus sinless must have been, so to speak, the Beginning of a fresh creation of God, and cannot have been linked just simply as all other human children with at most only holy, in general sinful, never sinless, ordinary human beings. This is doubtless the deepest reason also for all the honour paid to His Mother.

(ii.) *As to the Eucharistic Bread and Wine turned into the Body and Blood of Christ.* I take it that what repels her here is this apparent treating Christ as though He were divisible, and a divisible *thing*, and as though we literally ate and drank parts of Him. But any such notion is excluded by the very general doctrine of "concomitance" (=going together), by which, Christ, being not dead but alive, not a thing or things, but a Person: where His (risen and glorified) Body and Blood are, there also are His soul and His Divinity, each penetrating, and interpenetrated by, the other. The reasons why, especially in St. John's Gospel, chapter vi., the Body and the Blood, and the eating and drinking, are so strongly emphasised is to ensure the very important faith in the strict and entire reality of Our Lord's Presence—a reality greater or different from His ordinary Presence in our hearts—a reality closely connected with the physical eating and the physical drinking of those species—the Eucharistic elements. *Of course* it is possible to have too carnal a conception of the meaning of this doctrine. Yet I do not doubt that—upon the whole—the danger lies far more in an evaporation of the Presence into no more than the universal Presence of Christ, or even into a mere vague subjective thought of Him *as though* present.

## Baron Friedrich von Hügel

(iii.) *As to the difficulty of caring for, and of fervently attending, Matins or Evensong.* I quite understand it, I think. But I would dearly love to see you battle quietly against it, whilst using every reasonable means to enliven your attention and interest. If the services are somewhat long, yet their contents, especially the Psalms are admirable. Why not get to understand the Psalter *very* well? I mean not simply more or less by heart, but, on the contrary, by learning to see more clearly and more constantly the original meaning, the first state of soul, in them. You will get in a few days from me the late Canon Driver's beautifully precise re-translation from the Hebrew of all the Psalms — each printed on the page opposite to that on which the Revised Psalter stands printed. I should love you very slowly and ruminatingly to go through the whole — perhaps slightly marking with pencil under the words of the Psalms, in your Prayer Book, where Driver has taught you the precise original meaning where the Prayer Book text is obscure. This would bring rich life and deep feeling into them, or rather would reveal to you the life and the feeling. Our own Mass and Benediction, and especially Vespers and Compline, are, of course, filled with various Psalms. So also for understanding our, the great old Latin services, a sound knowledge of the Psalter is very useful. Then I look forward to the days, off and on, when with others, you would have a companion at these services. This would break and limit the isolation a good bit.

...

These difficulties are all so many additional special reasons for your holding out, even if you mostly have to go alone. But, Sweet, you would, of course, practise moderation in the matter; going, as you do, to Holy Communion at least once a week, and praying by yourself, as you do, in your little church by yourself. I do not see that you need have more than Evensong on the Sundays: that is supposing you get Holy Communion every Sunday morning.

And now at last I come to the biggest thing in your letter: what you say about liberty, freedom, in the Roman Catholic Church. I sadly realise that, given my remarks, or rather given the sheer fact of my raising the point to you at all the other day, you could not—at least if you followed me then in your usual sweetly receptive way—think at all differently. For if your own freedom would not, by becoming a Roman Catholic, get curtailed, where would be the object of my raising the point to you at all? It *must* have concerned yourself; and if it did not concern you, where lies the excess in your conclusion, from, indeed in, your simple reproduction of my words? I see this quite plainly, Child. But I soon felt very uncomfortable, you gone, as to what I had said. I know I spoke with edge and concentration, and I have waited anxiously to see its reception by you. Be a dear child now, and drop what I said then, attending simply to what I will write now.

First then, there can be no serious question of any curtailment of any right and reasonable freedom—such freedom as you practise now in your reading, studying, thinking—if ever you became a Roman Catholic. I have deliberately gone through all the duties, all even the chances and influences that would then surround you, and I can discover no such curtailment, either certain, or even probable.—Of course, you would yourself have a wide choice of confessors, devotions, spiritual books, religious habits; and if you yourself chose, or you let yourself go to vehement reaction against all your past, even where (as, thank God, it is) very good and wise: you could work your appurtenance to the Church in an impoverishing way. But that would be your own doing; and already you see far too plainly how central must always be and remain the dropping of all excess and vehemence, for such a danger to be at all near or likely. If you were a man, and a critical historian and philosophical thinker, and these activities occupied with religion, not simply reproductive or selective, but original and reconstructive, the question of freedom would occur. But note, my Sweet, that not only *it does not — it really does not —* occur for yourself: it gets answered by me, with whom it does, it cannot but occur, in the sense opposite to that in which you answer it for yourself. I deliberately admit *some* difficulty, *some* complication for such as myself; but I do not cease, thank God, to see and experience that the gain of my Roman Catholic appurtenance is, even simply for the solidity of my freedom, for the balance and reality of my outlook — *just simply even to my life of scholarship and thinking* IMMENSE. I know it is. So that I am sure that you are doubly removed from any real curtailment of your liberty, if ever you came to the Roman Catholic Church: for you are not a scholar, a thinker, by profession — and, even if you were, you could, and ought, and would gain a depth *and breadth* of rich liberty beyond what you could acquire elsewhere. You can see that, as to men like myself, this is my real conviction. How else could you explain my always keeping open in my mind the possibility and desirableness of Professor Norman Kemp Smith, of Edinburgh, coming to us later on?

Do not, Sweet, misunderstand any of this as a plea, as even the most indirect pressure for your changing. No: it has nothing to do with *that.* Only deep, strong, most clear calls of conscience would make it right for you to think of such a change. I only want, if God will bless this old bungler, to remove a false impression — I do not want, if ever such a condition of conscience arose, for you to be stopped from following it up by a *bugbear,* alas, of my own suscitation. You will, Blessing, if you truly can say so, give me an immense relief by telling me that you now understand. I will, of course, gladly explain further, if there is anything seriously obscure. I see that there was a double self-seeking about me that evening. I was thinking of my own case, instead of yours—and I was thinking of my own case unmanfully, softly, complainingly. As a matter of fact I have found, and I have at this moment, masses of deepest sympathy, even of a purely personal kind, and this not simply from dry scholars, but from darling Catholic saints of God. If I got more, it would turn my old head.

And now, my Child, one good hug, and another good hug, and a third good hug. And Christ bless you, guard you, expand, pacify, and give you genial Joy, here, now, and for ever.

Loving old Fatherly One,
H.

13 VICARAGE GATE

*28 February 1921*

Delighted by your letter and will now try and drop all that distress on that point from my mind. Of course you may copy parts or all of that L.S.S.R. paper of mine. You have never mentioned receiving a proof of a review of mine of a book by Heiler on *Prayer*. You are meant to keep *that. As* to St. Francis de Sales, I will send you some. Perhaps his chief work at once, the *Traité de L'Amour de Dieu*. I somewhat fear your finding him a bit cloying. I hope you will not, for his substance is admirable. How many souls he has trained to sanctity! But I want you still to read two short Fénelons—his *Education des Filles* and his chaplain's account of his daily life at Cambrai—the man lives there before one. Also Shakespeare—I too place *Macbeth* highest for spiritual insight—though *Lear* I take to be one of the most awful evidences of power of all three tragedies. But I like to keep the four tragedies compared—surely *Othello* stands almost as high spiritually as *Macbeth?*

F.v.H.

## Baron Friedrich von Hügel

13 VICARAGE GATE, W. 8

*1 March 1921*

Still tied to bedroom, but was able this morning to finish selection of Old Testament passages for my book.

Once and again was immensely struck and impressed with the richness, reality, penetrating spirituality of the Psalter, the Psalms at their best, a pity that frequent use — imperfect translation — and the backward elements (vindictiveness, earthly rewards — nebulousness as to the other life) so largely obscure these very magnificent things. — Will have a lovely Easter book to suggest.

*4 March.* Still in bedroom — the obstinate chest cold and cough upon the whole better, but still far from gone. Worst is, that not getting out leaves brain extra wearyable.

Thanks for Fénelon returned. Glad you are keeping the *Lettres Spirituelles* a bit. What utterly alive things they are! Like all the finest results of immense training, cost, perseverance, grace, they stand there as though they could not be otherwise — as if anyone, everyone thought it all!

Have just accepted to speak at a large Summer School at Swanwick on Sunday, 3 July. — Will try to get them to accept some quite definite point for my discourse.

13 VICARAGE GATE, W. 8

*11 April 1921*

Child of my old Heart,

Here is your book back. If you re-read your copy of my (Notes) on Holy Communion you will find it much more intelligible, I am sure. You had copied: carefully, but my poor text was rough!

Dare not write properly till after 2 May, as I explained on post card. — But one or two post cards will perhaps get written, and I can, of course, always gladly read letters

111

from you. Everything, *everything* once, sweetened in the love of God — of Christ

> que rien ne t' épouvante,
> que rien ne te trouble;
> Tout passe; Dieu seul.[6]
>
> S.Teresa.

What jolly good stuff those saints give one, don't they? Loving old Uncle-Father,

H.

13 VICARAGE GATE, KENSINGTON, W. 8

*Ascension Day, 5 May 1921*

Here at last I am more free again, and the first letter I write because I love to write it, is to my most dear little old Thing — though really "little," at least physically! is not the right word.

It was only late on Thursday night, 3rd, that the big strain came to an end, through the delivery of my address on "Suffering in God." The thing was, as it were, externally a success: twenty-six of us met together — a large number for our not large society. And they were all, as ever, most kind and dear to me personally. But I trust it is sincerely so — one feels, on such occasions, more cheered by agreement in the convictions expressed, than by any amount of such pleasant attentions. Some twelve of my listeners spoke through my machine after and on the paper; and only two agreed with my fundamental — to me such a clear, dear, and important point: that although, of course, God is full of sympathy and care for us; and though we cannot succeed vividly to represent His sympathy otherwise than as a kind of suffering, we must not

---

[6] French: May nothing frighten you,
May nothing trouble you;
Everything passes; God alone.

112

press this to mean that suffering, what we experience in our own little lives as suffering, is *as such* and *literally* in God. God is overflowing Love, *Joy*, and Delectation. I showed, I think, many and grave reasons as warnings against importing, or admitting suffering in God. I gave a detailed instance of ruin effected in a fine mind, and in all his outlook, in a man who began with that one eccentricity — real, literal suffering in God.

My Sweet: in a few days I am beginning the third and final writing of this thing; and when it is all typed and ready to go, for printing, to America — to be out in September — I shall want you to read it carefully for me, telling me if it comes home to you throughout as live and true, and if it is as clear as I can make it. I hope to have it thus ready, say, in three weeks from now.

And of course I shall greatly love seeing you here next Wednesday, 11th. As an exception, it happens that on that day the morning — say ten-thirty to twelve-thirty — would do quite well, so if afternoon would have to be shorter as to your visit, come in morning. If afternoon will really do as well, then I prefer afternoon — say four, or four-thirty, or five — for, I hope, an hour and a half.

13 VICARAGE GATE, KENSINGTON, W. 8

*19 May 1921*

Darling Child,

I find I can scribble a bit this afternoon, so I will write you a letter, Dear. You gave me no coming address, so I will just send this to Friendly Green, where you may still be. At least, they will forward all right, I do not doubt.

As to the Parallel Psalter book, I had to wait, because for months I was £100 and then £150 to the *bad* at the bank; but these last weeks I have been, to my pleased surprise, £150 to the *good. So* I could well afford this book for you, and got it at once, with such joy!

I well understand what you feel about religion, suffering and caring. But please notice carefully, and for a general principle of wise judgment, that religion, on its human side, in so far as it is a human activity—is subject to excesses and defects, to diseases and aberrations more or less special to itself but which no more prove anything against religion at its best—religion as it is on God's side—than do the corresponding excesses and defects, deflections and diseases of Art, of Science, of Politics, of Marriage, prove aught against these kinds of life and of reality, taken at their best and in their intendedness on God's side. I possess a French medical psychologist's very instructive yet dangerously plausible, really anti-religious book, *Les Maladies du Sentiment Religieux*. As a matter of fact, for his mind (perhaps unbeknown to himself) religion, the whole of religion, is these "maladies." We live in times of such obvious transition, decline, poverty of deep, creative conviction, of such excess of analysis over synthesis—that it is in the air all around us to ask questions, to poke about, to wonder, to drift, to use the microscope; where to become and to be, to produce reality, to adore and to will, and to see things in the large and upon the whole, and at their best, is what we all require.

As to religion and caring for our dear ones, I enclose for you to keep the glorious profession of faith and of love of St. Bernard on occasion of the death of his half-brother and fellow-Cistercian (=strict Benedictine) monk Gerard. The entire sermon is most touching. But is not this bit vibratingly beautiful? I have translated it as well as I could; but it has lost, alas, a good deal in the process!

I shall not be sending you, Sweet, that "Suffering and God" address, at least not typed, after all. I found on reflection, and after getting some letters from hearers of it, that it was little or no use to publish the thing as it stands—that it really requires, for such as do not already hold its views, an entire new section, a section i. which

114

would draw out the right principles and proper method for such an inquiry. You see, my Sweet, young people always just go ahead on such points, as though they were talking, say, of Sargent's portraits or of Drinkwater's plays, or at least of things which we can hold, overlook, comprehend. But as to God, we can, indeed, be sure, very sure, of Him—He is implied in all our thinking, feeling, willing, doing; it is the implicit faith in the reality and the useful work of truth, of goodness of life which will never die out for long amongst mankind. And we can, we do, gain vivid experience of Him, if only we will die, die, day and night, to self. We can thus increasingly *apprehend* Him—can know really about Him, the head, the source of all reality and of all sense of reality. But we cannot encircle Him, map Him out, exhaustively explain Him. We cannot really say, as these objectors cheerfully argued: "If He feels joy, He must also feel pain": we cannot, for we thus assume that we are dealing with a fellow human being; that by "feeling" in God we mean no other, no more, than by "feeling" in man. Nor can we argue, as another pressed upon me, that *he* would break his heart, if his only son took to an impure life; how much more then must God break His heart, if and when any of us gravely sins. We cannot so argue, because here again we do not encircle, penetrate God; and because we must not press points in ways and degrees which would contradict certain other, and really deeper, intimations and requirements of the religious sense. Now the deepest intimation and requirement we really have got—though sadly weakened in many of us by the fever and rush of life since about A.D. 1790— is Being (as distinct from Becoming), is Perfection (as distinct from Attempting), is indeed Action, but not Change. *Of course* change in ourselves, in the sense of becoming better and better in all things; but this—this need of change in us, comes simply from our imperfection. We are not God. Yet how we need Him! And this, then, not as just a larger ourselves, not as a larger Becoming, but as Being, as Joy Pure and Undefiled.

Now this, with the St. Bernard which I will now copy for you, must do for to-day, my Child.

13 VICARAGE GATE

*30 May 1921*

Am now, Child, in midst of proof correction of my *Essays,* as well as (when these leave me a pause) at work on the book. So I dare not write a long letter — only something to go with the accompanying MS. of *Suffering and God.* I am rather ashamed to lend, even you, this still not sufficiently clarified thing. Show it to no one else. You may, I trust, learn from it, even so. I have had further adhesions to its main positions.

I have been very happy over the thought of your visit to Mrs. Rice, a real short holiday. So glad peace is reigning within. How wise the *Imitation* is, in always preparing the soul for its desolate times; for if once we learn, and continue to learn better and better, how to keep on steadily during those times and to profit by them, why we have learnt the secret of solid advance.

Mrs. L — has written from America. Evidently going on steadily and well. She will, I believe though, grow richer in soul and outlook.

I will have to attend D. Farquhar's address before our L.S.S.R. meeting on 7 June, about Indian Pantheism — as soon as ever his reaches me. A great scholar for the *Indian* side of the question — but strangely inferior as soon as ever he comes to treat of the Christian positions. This, though he is a devoted Christian missionary, with at least thirty years of Christian religious thinking behind him. Why is this? I am sure of the answer. Because as a Protestant Nonconformist, he looks at all the Christian side from far too individualistic, sectarian, single Bible-texts, point of view. You cannot get these great questions solved, or even only stated greatly — except through much history, institutions, Church appurtenances. No doubt these things will not, alone, suffice; they can even be taken in a way that stifles. Yet they *are* wanted. A child may cut itself with the table-knife, yet such a knife is necessary for cutting the bread.

Trust no headaches, Child.

Loving old,

Uncle.

13 VICARAGE GATE, KENSINGTON, W. 8

*21 July 1921*

Child Mine,

I have now lots to answer, lots to tell. But first about the books. I am sending you three books about *Socrates* — two are presents, one is a loan; and a fourth book as a help — an adviser — with regard to sensitiveness.

1. I want you first to read John Burnet's analysis of the evidence as to Socrates, and *his* estimate as to the influences which played upon Socrates's mind, and the way in which he sorted them out and developed them. You will find this in Burnet's edition of Plato's *Phædo* (which I lend you), pages ix-lvi. I want you to study these pages twice through, most carefully.

2. Then take (in the volume I give you of Xenophon's *Anabàsis* and *Memorabilia*) the "Memorabilia of Socrates," pages 349-507. This, too, I want read through at least twice (with the notes, as far as you can follow these; and looking up all sites in your *Classical Atlas*). Please keep alive everywhere to Socrates's *irony*; he hardly ever opens his mouth without it colouring what he says; take him literally and you mostly make him say the very opposite he means. Try, too, to trace the influence of the Sophists, of Anaxagoras, of the Pythagoreans and Orphics, etc.:

117

Burnet ought to have helped you towards this. And finally contrast his teachings and tone with the Christians' outlook.

3. Then take the *Four Socratic Dialogues of Plato*, translated by Jowett with Preface by Edward Caird, which I give you. – First, a double reading of Caird's Preface, pages v-xi. Then the Analysis of the "Eúthyphro," pages 1-9. Then the "Eúthyphro" itself, pages 10-36, twice. The same with the "Apology," the "Crito" *(Creito)* and the *Phædo.* – Note again in these four *Dialogues*, Socrates's irony, the sources of his ideas, and their limits and peculiarities – when compared with Xenophon's account of them, and still more when compared with the Christian outlook. (Of course pre-existence is a myth, and there do not really occur any memories from such a pre-existence.)

When you have done all this, I should like you to re-read again Burnet's account, and to see how far you yourself have found it true. (You will remember that I utilised Burnet's elucidation of all that the *philosopher* Socrates owed to the *religious* (Pythagorean and Orphic), in my criticism of Corrance, and his turning from the Sun, definite religion, to the Moon, philosophy.)

4. I give you Faber's *Spiritual Conferences* because, although I do not believe him to be a truly classical spiritual writer, several of these conferences will – at least can, I think – help you much. I am thinking especially of "Kindness," 1-53; "Wounded Feelings," 260-74; "The Monotony of Piety," 314-32; and "All Men have a Special Vocation," 375-96. Surely, Sweet, there is much, much knowledge of our poor human heart here. I feel that Faber's limitations are, at bottom, three. (i.) He hardly ever leaves anything to his hearers or readers to develop further by and for themselves. He was cleverly called "the spiritual Dickens" by a man who pointed out the same peculiarity in Dickens. (ii.) He has got a touch – indeed more than a touch – of vulgarity – he can, at times, speak as

though he were a Salvation Army Hallelujah lass. And (iii.) he never quite got beyond the anti-Protestantism so common amongst our converts—devotion to the Blessed Virgin, loyalty towards the Pope, and the like, were, because antipathetic to Protestants, underlined by, revelled in by, Faber to a degree which, at times, put them out of their Catholic proportion, their Catholic perspective. He would thus, instead of a continuator of the grand old pre-Reformation Catholic piety of England, become an imitation—an affectation—of Italian, of Neapolitan piety. But you will find only little of all this in this volume, I think. Faber sprang from an originally French, Huguenot family; hence, in part, I do not doubt, his love of point, paradox, hyperbole.

As to your news and questions, Dear.

There is, to my delight, once more your fundamental experience of, and call to Recollection—the Prayer of simple Quiet. This is, of course, a true, deep grace of God; it is by being very faithful to it, by feeding it, by dropping what weakens or drives it away, that you will become happy and holy. How beautifully simple! I quite understand the two stages of it—the stage of distractions and of having to drive—to strive to drive them away; and then the stage of a living, somehow self-acting recollection—with God, His peace, power and presence, right in the midst of this rose of spiritual fragrance.

I think you could pretty easily weaken, or delay, this sense by too much dwelling (even from the best of motives) upon the criticisms of yourself, such as you mention. I do not believe in getting peace from seeking (and even finding) that the criticism was not deserved. And indeed even if it was entirely not deserved, our minding criticism so very much—its hurting us so much: this is surely a weakness, a faulty condition, at least of our nerves. If and when we become genuinely deeply humble, we shall feel that we very certainly are full of faults, either those particular faults, or other faults—it will be too much of a most certain fact to our minds, for any possible, or even obvious mistake as to the fault—the kind of fault—to surprise or vex us out of our peace. Still, of course, even then—then especially—we would quietly and shortly look as to whether we can find the fault in us, and if we found it would ask Christ Our Lord to help us weed it out or drop it. Yet always would I expect to find you to grow more by feeding the quiet within you than by direct self-examinings or self-fightings. These two latter things also to exist in your life—but much less, less centrally than the feeding of the quiet and the loving of God, Christ, and others in it.

As to *Confession*, I have a certain complication about it in my mind, which, I expect, is not very common even amongst my own people. You see, with the Sacraments, as, indeed, with all other points of religion, I so love to trace the great lines of their development, and to find out, and to cling to, whatever may be of the essence of the Catholic doctrine and practice. Applying this to Confession I find (as you can read in full in my *Mystical Element*) that the essential, primitive, unchangeable part is *obligatory* Confession in case of *Grave Sin*. The Protestant Reformers abolished the *Obligation* in any and every instance. And now High Churchmen have come to recommend fairly frequent Confession, in imitation of our (R.C.) late mediaeval, and still more, our modern habit. Now I do not doubt that fairly frequent Confession can help on souls, yet I love to keep quite clear in my own mind an element of *Obligation* which the Protestant Reformers unhappily lost—abolished; and an element of Conditionality—Freedom—with regard to the late mediaeval and modern Frequent Confession, which even my High Anglican friends are lacking in. I want, in this point also, a wise, firm circumspection. But to take the practice of Confession as simply in all circumstances not obligatory—as always what we call "Confession of Devotion," I quite see that also taken this way, the soul can get real help and growth in self-knowledge, humility, etc., from it. Since *our*, late centuries, discipline in the matter is just disciplinary — i.e. since Rome herself could relax it any way up to, excluding, Confessions for Grave Sin, it is certainly not for me to press you to very frequent Confessions of Devotion. I myself go every fortnight or every three weeks — but this, simply because of the extant *discipline* of the Church, and because I feel I ought not to exempt myself from it. I expect that every six months would be quite frequent enough for yourself, to get all the good, in your particular life and particular *attrait*, that the practice would be likely to give you. Of course, you would have to learn to do so with a special kind of freedom and a special kind of strictness according to the special demands of God upon your soul. *Cela varie*, Huvelin would have said, *entre âme et âme.*[7]

I have, these last days, been seeing a former fellow student of Gertrude's, for many years an Agnostic, then a fervent High Anglican; who, now thirty-eight, is inclining to take herself back, to look out for No. 1. to grumble and to turn sour. Am doing what I can for her: pray for her. Have explained how she requires a second conversion — this time against the dust and drear when the physical enthusiasm dwindles.

The American, Miss Branham, who went to try her call, with those strict, field-working Benedictinesses, has just written to say she is very happy as a hardworked Postulant; I really think she will succeed: a fine instance of the genuineness of such calls.

I do wish those headaches would go. Will tell Thekla what you say for her when I see her.

---

[7] French: "This varies ... between soul and soul."

*27 July 1921*

My darling Gwen-Child,

Let me now try first to explain about *Confession*. You see, the very earliest Christian position as to grave (="Mortal") sin was that a man or woman, one baptised as an adult (and thereby purified from his or her sins), did not again fall into such grave sins. Hence the question as to what he or she should do, in case they *did*, in fact, relapse, did not then arise.

(You can find traces of these conditions and convictions in *Saint John's Epistles*, and other nooks and corners of the New Testament.) But I need not tell you that only a little time was, in most regions of the nascent Church, necessary for this first intense martyr fervour to abate, and for the question concerned to become very much alive and fully practical. If you look in *Tertullian* (perhaps the selection you possess would suffice, but anyhow in others of his writings he is quite plain), you will find "the second plank after shipwreck" — the "first plank" being baptism. What *is* "the second plank"? "The second plank" is Christian Penance or Penitence. Of what does this consist? It consists of three parts, *each of which in case of grave* (=mortal) *sin, is necessary for the Divine Forgiveness*: contrition, confession, and satisfaction. The meaning of "contrition" is, of course, quite clear; then, as now, it means a definite sorrow for having committed those sins, a sorrow from the motive of the love of God, and a deliberate, firm resolution of amendment! The meaning of "satisfaction," too, remains substantially the same — the restoration, as far as possible, of whatever we may have unjustly taken away — conjugal fidelity, or health, or fortune, etc. — but the "confession" then meant, for several centuries, a *Public* confession, in the Christian Church Assembly, before, and

122

into the hands *of the Bishop*. The bishop it was who, during the earlier time, only after a considerable space filled with works and proofs of penitence, solemnly, again in the Christian Church Assembly, reconciled the sinner with God—absolved him from his sins, in the name and by the power of Christ.

Now in those early centuries *there was no habit of confession for venial sins*. I suppose that now and then such a thing as private confession for venial sins happened. But if it did, it must have been rarely, since I do not know of any documents attesting such confessions. In any case, it is entirely clear that such confessions were not considered obligatory—were not believed to be essential to reconciliation with God. The proof of this is that even the strictest Roman Catholic theologians to this hour teach that we cannot press strict obligation to beyond grave (=mortal) sins; that the confession of venial sins (such as has become general in the Roman Catholic Church since, say, A.D. 1350 or a little earlier) can only be pressed on the ground of its being conceited not to follow the prevalent discipline of the Church, and on the ground of the spiritual utility, etc. In strictness, even with us Roman Catholics, a soul which has committed no grave sin—is not conscious of an unconfessed grave sin—would not be obliged to more than to present itself, once a year, at Eastertide, to the priest, to tell him it had no grave sin to confess, and to ask his blessing (even this only because of certain Decrees of Councils in about 1260 and 1560).

Now confessions for venial sin we call confessions of *Devotion*—confessions for mortal sin we call confessions of Obligation. My feeling I somehow *must* go to confession (for venial sin) does not make such confession into a confession of obligation; nor contrariwise, does my not feeling any obligation to confess unconfessed mortal sin make such confession into a confession of devotion. What the

123

Church thinks, not what you or I feel or think, is here decisive and discriminative.

Now for myself, upon the whole, I regret, I will not say all confessions of devotion; I believe, on the contrary, that they have helped to train and sanctify many a soul. Also, I am glad that Anglicans should practise them—in moderation and wisely. But what I mind much more is the breach at the Reformation, by the Protestant reformers, even in England—the breach, not in the then prevalent practice of confessions of devotion, but in the immemorial doctrine and conviction of *confessions of obligation*. It was then that the conviction was abandoned that a Christian (if he have the physical opportunity of finding a priest) cannot attain forgiveness for mortal sin, without confession, as one of the three essential conditions of Christian Penitence.—True, the fathers of Anglicanism managed, most wisely, to retain the doctrine and practice of confession, for all souls which spontaneously wanted it, which felt it would help them. And again I do not doubt that many a High Churchman has in his heart of hearts continued the old pre-Reformation, Catholic conviction of the *necessity*, the *obligation*, of confession *in case of grave sins*. Yet, alas, this is not the official position—he is not free to press it—confession remains, officially, even for grave sin —amongst Anglicans—less obligatory than, amongst Roman Catholics, is confession for venial sin (for here, as explained, there is the fear of going against the present discipline of the Church, etc.).

So you can now understand, I hope, my Child, what I meant in this whole matter. It seems to me that, for yourself, you will do well by using confessions of devotion in moderation and with wisdom and peacefulness; and that (if you can do so without strain and mental contortion) it will be well if you can add to this practice the conviction that, if you had grave sin on your conscience, you would then be *bound* to confess.—You see, this, as regards your own practice of confession, introduces no complication of any kind. It only somewhat complicates your *Anglican* outlook. And, Blessing, the cry of my old heart is to be — to become — a not all unworthy follower of Him who broke not the bruised reed and quenched not the burning flax! — so there, enough about *that!*

My holiday begins *certainly* on 11 August, possibly on 8 August (i.e. if they have me at Farnham Castle from 8 August to 11 August—when I join Eva and Pucky at Thursley). I have written to the bishop proposing, as an alternative, to come to them *after* Thursley, i.e. from Friday, 9 September, to Monday, 12 September.

Am trying hard to get you a good second-hand copy of Jowett's Plato translation complete. It is in *that* that I intend to march you through certain dialogues for Plato himself, when you have done the Socrates reading.

Loving Uncle.

About Harry's book—another time.

13 VICARAGE GATE, W. 8

*29 July 1921*

My darling Gwen,

Thanks much for letter.

1. About confession, then, we have got all clear. I am feeling that it will be a good thing for you to go to the amount you propose, also for the reason that it still further forms you along the lines of the moderate, *Church* mystical, the mixed type—by far the safer and richer. That very balanced, wide-seeing American psychologist of religion, whom I saw in his room some days back, is full of the all-importance of the difference between Pure or Sheer or Exaggerated Mysticism (which is akin to Pantheism or some kinds of Spiritualism) and Mixed or Moderate Mysticism, which finds its completion, articulation and safety in history and institutions. The latter Mysticism both gives

to, and gets from, history and institutions much, very much.

2. About the Sadhu: I enclose the memorandum I drew up, at the request of Canon Streeter and Mr. Appasamy, towards the construction and orientation of their book on the Sadhu. I was much struck with how far more rich and probing the outlook was of the young Indian layman, the son of Indian converts to Christianity, than the Englishman, a cleric — a canon of an historic Christian church, and descended from a long Christian ancestry — a man middleaged, too. It was Appasamy who — how often — was and is puzzled by the Sadhu's insistence upon direct inspiration — that he does nothing except under such. "But please, Baron, is this necessary? Cannot, and does not God speak to us also through various means which spring from Him?" The canon — a man whom I like, he is so clean and so serious, and so pacific and sweet in discussion — would never ask such a question; indeed I doubt not that his chief interest in the Sadhu springs from this Indian, and, *in some ways*, supremely individualist, attitude. I say "in some ways," for, after all, his mind and words are — most fortunately for all — saturated with what he finds in the New Testament.

I find the Sadhu to be a fine, firm character — a devoted will, but to have curiously little mind. I think if he had more mind (and remained as finely unfanatical as he now is) he could not think, say, the following strangely unperceptive thoughts. For one thing, he told me himself, upon my questioning him very carefully on the point that, during the thirteen years since he has been a Christian, he has *never*, not even for some moments, experienced spiritual dryness, spiritual desolation. I asked my close friend, Professor N. Kemp Smith, the philosopher, a religious mind, what he thought of this, and without hesitation he judged that the Sadhu either did not really know himself, or did not know what "spiritual desolation" means, or did not understand either. Then, as to the continual Direct Inspiration, I was lent one of his addresses, typed, in which he specially insisted upon this point; yet much the most alive thing in the whole address was the exclamation: "He made us for Himself, and restless is our heart until it rests in Him," which very certainly comes from St. Augustine's *Confessions*, Book 1. chapter i. section 1.

3. As to Suggestion and Auto-Suggestion and Religion, or at least Mystical Religion, you can find in my *Mystical Element* certain positions, taken over from M. Boutroux, which I still believe to be sound. Also please read, and lend if and where this may be wise, Father Walker on "The Psychology of the Spiritual Exercises," in the *Hibbert Journal* for last April, which I also send (pages 401-13 there).

(I also enclose the *Hibbert Journal* for this July, because of the symposium in it on "Morals and Religion." I *think* you have not yet seen my little paper there, pages 605-10. Professor Chevalier, pages 610-15, I like, though it is perhaps too, as it were, mathematically clear. But the other three papers are very unsatisfying, I think.)

4. Dearie, I have plenty of money just now, so want to tip you a five pounds for any little outing or what not. Here it is—bless you! I heard from the bishop yesterday, I am to come to them from 8 August to 11 August.

After all I had better send the two *Hibberts* in a separate parcel. You see, Dear, the all-important points as to Suggestion, Auto-Suggestion, Mono-Ideism, etc. are to remember (i.) that all such things, where real and fruitful, are means, methods, connections, etc.—instrumental; and (ii.) that they can be thus real and fruitful because there exist realities—above all The Reality—distinct from them and us. Religion, as such, makes straight for these latter things; Psychology, etc. may, and does, potter over those other, lesser things.

*Letters to a Niece*

13 VICARAGE GATE

*8 August 1921*

My Gwen-Child,

Before starting to-day for my holiday, I write down this scheme of the study of this Jowett's *Plato* for you. It will go with the volumes—your own copy—as soon as such copy is found by my booksellers.

I divide up *Plato* into five groups and periods—and of these I want you to take the greatest dialogues in four of these groups and periods. (One of the groups is too hard for any but specialists.)

I. Socratic Dialogues. *Eúthyphro—Apology. Crito. Phædo.* You have already done these.

II. Educational Dialogues.

1. *Protagoras.*

2. *Gorgias.*

3. *Phædrus.*

4. *Meno.*

5. *Symposium.*

Omit the Critical Dialogues.

Read Comprehensive Dialogues—*Phædo* really belongs here. *The Republic. Work of old age. The Laws.*

I should like you always to study Jowett's Introduction carefully—then the Dialogues *twice*; and then the Introduction a last time.

Please specially watch, in the *Phædrus*, the *Meno*, the *Symposium* and the *Republic*, points taken over later by the Christian thinkers—especially St. Augustine.

I incline to recommend your beginning with the Socratic Dialogues again, and reading them here for the purpose, not of Socrates but of Plato—and reading these so as to keep the *Phaedo* in its place according to the date of composition.

## Baron Friedrich von Hügel

THE RED LION INN, THURSLEY, NEAR GODALMING, SURREY

23 *August 1921*

My darling Gwen-Child,

At last I am scribbling to you again, with plenty to say, but still in a drifting, lazy, tired holiday mood, hence shrinking away from much detail or precision. Let me number my subjects.

1. Before leaving home, I wrote you a letter of instructions as to the exact selection, order, method, etc., with which I should like you to read *Plato*; and this letter I left with my lady bookseller, to put into the parcel of Jowett's *Plato* — four volumes — as soon as they had received a well-preserved and not overdear second-hand copy (the book has been out of print a long while now). You will see that I assume you to have carefully studied the Socratic Dialogues (including the Phædo, which really belongs to a later period of writing); that I group for you the other dialogues which I want you to study into four groups; and that I invite you to skip — for the present at least — the six very difficult and technical dialogues of the *critical* group. Even so, you have a large and splendidly rich field before you, and we will talk over together, and read certain great passages together, carefully, I hope and believe. I want you to get to think and feel Platonically on quite a number of points.

2. I left home on Monday, 8th, and stayed at Farnham Castle till after tea on the 11th. How full up, and what a *va et vient*[8] it was, and, apparently, always is there! The widow of an Episcopalian Bishop of Glasgow and her daughter; another golden-haired young lady, and Walter Frere, an old friend of mine, head of the Community of the Resurrection at Mirfield, Yorks, there — the ladies till

---

[8] French: "going and coming"

Wednesday morning, Frere till Thursday morning. Then on Wednesday, from eleven till six, some sixteen clerics, suffragan bishops, canons, rectors, etc., for a conference on Faith Healing. Then by tea-time on Wednesday the Fords — the parents and the seven children. And on the Thursday by lunch-time, the Episcopalian Bishop of New York and two other gentlemen for the night. Miss Winnie Talbot and the secretary, Miss Wilcox, were there all the time.

3. ...

4. The bishop asked me to say a few words to those assembled Faith-Healing clerics, with two of whom I got some pleasant talk before and later on. I attempted three points. That I could not feel the force of the appeal to St. Paul's account of the faith-healers in the Church of Corinth, since there we have the uprush of a mass of forces and influences, strong with the strength of an immense new religion—forces and influences in no wise directly produced, or even intended, by St. Paul, but simply regulated, graduated by him, seeing that they existed in chaotic force all around him. He had not looked to see what the world then required, nor had lent an ear to what it asked for, and had then assumed the presence of these powers amongst his Christians. No: the powers were *there*, seethingly, obtrusively; because they were there, he organised and utilised them. — Did my hearers feel they possessed such powers? Were these their powers so strong as to demand regulation, graduation? If not, was it not *unreal* (surely, a great weakness in religion!) to organise, even to discuss, as though the demand for such things, or even the desirableness of such things, were equal to their supply, to their obtrusive presence? — That this my point was not controversially meant—that I should feel the same about my own people: I did not see indications of their possessing such *individual* faith-healing powers, and did not see how, unless and until they possessed them, it was *real* to discuss their utilisation. — My second point was

that I felt Extreme Unction, practised as it was amongst ourselves as a sacrament—officially and not as an individual gift—a rite so ancient as to be clearly taught in the New Testament, in the Epistle of St. James—to stand on quite a different plane. That I should love to see them work for the new recognition of this. Let them have the insight and the courage to part company with Luther's rejection of that Epistle, and to work for the acceptation of that touchingly beautiful, most helpful rite—the anointing of the dangerously sick. And my third point was to beware, in either case, of action parallel with that of the physician, or in supplantation of him. We are Christians, not Christian Scientists. The action of the physician should move upwards, from the body, his chief concern, to the mind—and with God in the background. The action of the priest should move downwards—from God as his central concern, to the human soul and the body at last. That is, let them strive to become, not faith-healers but saints. How I have learnt to see that even the tenderness, the social interest and sympathy of Christ, was so entrancing and so operative because proceeding from, and throughout conjoined with, a lofty sanctity, an awful holiness—the bending of loftiness, the mercy of purity: the two—not any one of these things—the two together—with the Holiness, the closest union of God as the starting and returning point of the whole Anecdote: how the Good Shepherd nuns attain to successes with fallen women, greater than any other body, whether Roman Catholic or not.

5. I should love to write on, but must now go to Puck—who has to be out of this inn. Am here till 9 September; then home. Poor Hillie has had a sudden violent attack of influenza—been very weak, but is mending now. Was moved to Vicarage Gate.

Loving Uncle-Father,
H.

*7 October 1921*

You bring up, my Gwen-Child, a point which I suppose you really feel an objection. Even if you do not feel it so, I think it well worth while to clear out this corner of your mind, so as to make quite sure that you correctly seize the truly great doctrine of Purgatory. I want, then, to make sure that you clearly understand that, according to that doctrine, suffering (*rightly accepted* suffering) is indeed usually necessary for, is inherent in, the purification from sin, evil habits, etc. But it makes no substantial distinction between such purification as taking place already here or taking place in the Beyond. In all our Retreats we are taught that it will have been our own fault, if the sufferings of our life here have not sufficed to purify us from our sins and evil habits. Of course, even very great sufferings would not, simply of themselves, purify us from even small evil habits. It is only suffering *meekly accepted, willed, transfigured by love of God, of Christ*—it is only such that will purify or cure anything. This is so true that, where the love is perfect, this *love alone, without any suffering* not directly prompted by itself completely blots out the evil dispositions. Such a soul, even if previously a great sinner, goes straight to Heaven upon its death. Yet in all cases, Purgatory applies indifferently to sufferings rightly borne in *this* life and the same similarly borne in *that* life. There is simply no such thing as a Purgatory here followed, as though it had not been, by a Purgatory hereafter.—On the contrary, every pang God allows to reach us here, and which we manage to bear a little well, does *a work not to be repeated.* We become thus fitter and fitter for complete union with Christ and God from the very minute of our death.

I have written "a little well" on purpose. For to suffer well is far more difficult than to act well (although the ordinary talk is that we have just "to grin and bear" suffering—we can do nothing to it or with it!!!). Holy suffering is the very crown of holy action. And God is no pedant: He can and does look to the substance of our suffering, and knows how to penetrate beyond our surface restlessness or murmurs. Indeed part of the grand work suffering effects in the soul doubtless springs from the way in which, when acute, it almost invariably humbles us: we can much less easily cut a fine figure in our own eyes over our sufferings, than we can over our actions when in peace and plenty.

You understand all the above completely, I trust? We will both do what gently, peaceably we can to have all our Purgatory—every drop of it—here; and then, and then, Heaven, the closest union, unfailing, with Pure Joy, with All Purity, with Christ, with God.

Loving old Uncle,

H.

### 13 VICARAGE GATE, W. 8

*12-14 November 1921*

My darling Gwen-Child,

Here I am, at last again scribbling to you! I do not know whether you have gone back to the old rectory; but I will address this there, unless I hear, before putting this up, that you are at some other given address.

I have much to say, as to *your* points, and a good many things about my own experience.

1. ...

2. I am delighted you have now read Plato's *Phædo* four times. How fine, if gradually, you get to know all the Dialogues (except those six or seven very technical ones) as well as this one! Margaret Roper, Sir Thomas More's daughter, doted upon *Plato* in the Greek original; I shall be glad indeed if my own Niece-daughter comes to know *Plato*, almost as well, in the English translation.

3. ...

4. I had three most happy, I hope useful, days at Beaconsfield. There were nine of us in all. Mr. W. B. Trevelyan,
the head of the house — a second cousin of C. M. Trevelyan
(who wrote on Wycliffe and Garibaldi); and his young
sub-warden — both very High Anglican clerics; then Mr.
Hockley, Rector of Liverpool, a tall, black-haired, manly
creature; also Mr. Carey, second-in-command of the Cow-
ley Fathers — a straight, simple man; a bishop returned,
after eighteen years' work in Bloemfontein (South Africa),
a year ago, a fatherly, genial man; a Mr. Platts, Vicar of
St. Michael's, a High Ritual church close to Thekla's convent — zealous, straight; and finally a charming layman,
Mr. Arthur Smallwood, Governor of Greenwich Hospital,
about forty years old, with whom I got some very private
talk. No; there was one man more: Father Denys, one of
the three Anglican Benedictines who did not go over to
Rome when, some fifteen years ago, the other twelve or so
of the community of Caldy did so. I like this Father Denys
much. I certainly think the position of a Benedictine not
accepting the jurisdiction of the Pope a very strange one.
But if "Charity covereth a multitude of sins," good faith
is compatible with, and expresses itself in a multitude of
strangely illogical positions. And deliberate self-renunciation is everywhere dear and darling. And then this Father
Denys is evidently a man of much spiritual shrewdness
and extraordinarily wide reading. They certainly gave me
lots to do. Half an hour's speech at the preliminary meeting — as to the precise order and spirit of our conference;
an address of one hour; and answers to questions on it,
for another hour, on the Wednesday — all as to facts about
God, specially useful to know in prayer; on Thursday,
address of an hour, and answers for an hour — both as regards the facts about the soul, most useful to know in
prayer. — And besides, I got some private talks with Mr.

Platts, Father Denys and Mr. Smallwood (as already said).

My chief general impressions were, I think, three. (i.) What clean, good, straight, humble, earnest men! My Gwen, you can add them, I am sure, all eight, to the list of thoroughly clean men I tried to make out for you the other day. (ii.) How greatly, even in a sense excessively, they were under the spell of Rome — the mighty Mother. I felt it in their attitude towards myself which was *very certainly* not only, not even chiefly, because of my individual personality, but because I was a Roman Catholic, trained in, and who could tell them about, that Mother Church. When I said just now, "excessive," I mean that I found them with little or no discrimination between what, with us, is the substance and unchangeable, and what is, again with us, the accident as the changing, or at least changeable, discipline of the Church.

And (iii.) that final question showed, I thought, that they attributed too much power to training, for they asked whether the spirit and life of an Abbé Huvelin should not be taught and trained into such Anglicans as were prepared for the clerical life, and especially those who were to have the care of souls. I answered that certainly it would be well, more and more to improve such preparation; but that I was confident such men as Huvelin would always be rare, anywhere and at all times. That he himself, e.g. had derived only a fragment of what he was and became, from his technical, seminary training; that I thought it would be well to teach the *average* Church student that there were — there existed — deep, rare souls, both amongst the laity and amongst the clerics, and to encourage such student to refer such rare lay-folk to the one or two deeply spiritual clerics be might be taught to know about. That if Anglicans managed to have, say, two such deeply spiritual clerics in each diocese, they should be esteemed richly favoured. That only great graces, many natural gifts, much suffering, and devoted heroism — all this or much of all this combined — would ever produce an Abbé Huvelin or a Curé d'Ars.

5. Have had a bad night, so must stop this my second go at this letter. May all be going well, or at least better with you, Child.

Loving old Father-Uncle,

Poor Muriel! But how brave she is being.

*From letter of 19 November 1921*

2. As to Socrates (=Plato) in the (*Protagoras*), you must not apologise for your dissatisfaction on those two points; for you are *right*, deeply right, about them. Indeed there is also a third point, about which Socrates (=Plato) here is equally mistaken or undiscriminative. Let me write the three points out clearly.

(i.) Courage=knowledge; indeed virtue of any kind= knowledge. This is certainly false, for the reasons you give. But you will have noticed that Socrates fully confesses that mankind at large does not take this view. Well — mankind at large was and is, on this point, closer to the facts, than Socrates or Plato. But, besides men generally, there were also ancient Græco-Roman thinkers and poets who felt and who taught the opposite — Ovid wrote:

Video meliora proboque;
Deteriora sequor?[9]

I see the better and I approve it; and (yet) I follow the worse. Yet it is Christianity, in the completion of the Hebrew prophetic religion, which, as against the Græco-Roman world generally, has established the full facts — has made me see and feel most vividly the difference between

---

[9] Latin: I see the better and I approve (it);
I follow the worse?

*Baron Friedrich von Hügel*

knowledge and virtue, between a clear head and a clean heart. On this point Kant is deeply Christian, when he insists upon the good will as supremely precious, and when, in his doctrine of Radical Evil, he holds that men can and do deliberately prefer evil to good.

(ii.) Socrates (=Plato) lumps, in his doctrine of opposites, two very different things hopelessly together. There is *(a)* the *contrary*, the different—say, blue and yellow, compared with red, among colours; or notes A, C, compared with D, among sounds. Here, two things, say two virtues, though distinct and different from each other, can yet, perfectly well, co-exist alongside of, or in union with, or fusion each with the other.

And there is *(b)* the *contradictory*, where one thing is the direct negation of the other; so with light, and absence of all light, etc. Here no one thing can, in any one and the same respect, contain, or be composed of, such contradictories. Thus, among the virtues, a man cannot, in precisely the same respect, be both courageous and cowardly.

(iii.) Socrates (=Plato) insists here on the good as just simply the pleasant; nor will he allow any action to be measured as to the morality except according as, at least eventually, it issues in pleasure or at least a surplusage of pleasure. Now here Socrates (=Plato) has not arrived at the profoundly important distinction between pleasure and beatitude (joy). He as yet does not see that evil doing, in certainly the greater number of cases, occurs simply because it is connected with some immediate pleasure; whereas, doing right is very frequently connected with the sacrifice of some immediate pleasure or the facing of some immediate pain—yet the yielding to sheer pleasure is the sure road to losing all beatitude, to losing even the sense of what it means. Whereas the resisting of sheer pleasure, according as right reason and duty may demand, is the sure road to joy.—I take it that Socrates (=Plato) not seeing this (iii.) is the chief cause why he

137

holds his (1). For if once we vividly perceive that virtue consists essentially in holding out against sheer pleasure for solid joy, and that evil doing consists essentially in yielding to sheer pleasure and thus losing solid joy; there is no need, there is no room, for knowledge, still less for the identity of knowledge with virtue. Yet note, Child, how these three errors are not errors pure and simple; but that they are stages on the way to precious truths. For: as to (1), it is true that there exists much *material* (=non-formal) evil doing; that men do what in itself is evil, often out of sheer ignorance that it is evil. And with his searching about for a knowledge as somehow close to virtue, Socrates (=Plato) is working his way towards a system of *objective* ethics — what, especially nowadays, we want again very badly. — As to (2), it is true that the several virtues have ultimately to be conceded as expressions, dispositions, effects, etc., of one and the same soul. Hence that, however different they may look, they must not be conceived as utterly unlike each other. — And as to (3), the end, the final measure, of virtue is indeed a state of soul the very opposite of unhappiness, constraint, disgust. Socrates (=Plato) is here after the supreme good, the utter joy, which, so far, he understates horribly by the petty term of pleasure.

So glad of your post card too, and that you have got to the *Gorgias.* You see that list I gave you will, if followed out, give you Plato *as he grows,* as he corrects himself. You will end by taking the mature Plato and correcting the immature Plato by the mature Plato, only that, no doubt, certain characteristically Hellenic weaknesses remain, more or less, to the end. E.g. of the above three points, No. (1) remains, in parts, to the very end; but not so No. (2) nor No. (3).

Loving old,
Uncle-Father.

*9 December 1921*

My darling Gwen-Child,

I have indeed been silent a long time — with, now, three dear and interesting letters of yours to answer. The reasons of this have been two. I have been a good deal tried by that arterial pressure at night; and as the doctor had told me that the less exertion there was in my day, the less I should suffer from it at night, I determined to try what cutting down everything at all avoidable would do. I am certainly now free from that pressure, or, at least, from those effects — though, I suspect, only for a little spell. Yet I am deeply thankful for it, since it means capacity for my composition work. My second reason was that I was trying to get you the *Curé d'Ars*, and that stupid postal losses — of the first order — have delayed my receiving the books till to-day. I now send you, as presents, the *Life of the Curé*, two volumes, and his *Spirit*, in one little volume. (The *Esprit* repeats in part the sayings registered in the *Vie*; but adds many fresh sayings.) I wanted to send you these volumes ready bound, but received them thus; and I think it better not first to get them bound, as you would then not have the books till after Christmas. I have cut the books open for you, as I believe myself to be expert at this. I trust and believe that the Curé's spirit will sink into your heart, and help you greatly on to geniality, humility, peace and happiness in God and for Him.

...

As to the young ex-curate, now one of our people: how difficult, indeed how impossible, it is to judge whether such extreme renunciation is quite sound in and for that particular soul, and will help it on to deep but quite balanced self-renunciation (as in Abbé Huvelin, the Curé d'Ars, etc.), or whether it is going to lead to dangerous reactions, etc. The Christian life, at its deepest and highest, is certainly not mere, not sheer, common sense. And yet—*in the long run*—*some* common sense has got to get into it, unless it is to come to grief—something like with visions and the excellent advice Edward Talbot gave you concerning them. There, too, one has just simply to wait, and, meanwhile, not to treat such things as central or as the measure of our advance or closeness to God.

As to whether converts to Rome are proselytisers. I think *at first, as a rule*, they are. Surely this is not difficult to understand. Such souls have generally come, with considerable sacrifices, and, at the time, with much spiritual light and fervour, to see and feel sure of various facts which they before saw fitfully or hardly at all. They very easily—all but inevitably—forget or overlook the not inconsiderable lights or helps they had before; and they have not yet been long enough in the old Church to have experienced its human poornesses nor to have themselves, within that Church, passed through desolation and reaction. My brother told me of an interesting conversation he had with our Bishop Brownlow, after the latter had been one of our priests and then a bishop some forty-eight years since he had been an Anglican High Church curate. My brother told him how he sometimes felt himself to be possibly quite wrong in not being more active and enterprising in trying to gain individual Protestants to the Church. That, as a matter of fact, he did nothing direct in this way—he never took the first step. The bishop answered that, after the first few years of his Roman Catholic life, when his zeal was restless and, he had now long thought, indiscreet, he also had never pressed anyone; had never taken the first step with anyone; that he had now seen for many a long year how easy it is to disturb souls from out of what contains much truth and which they *can* and *do* assimilate to their spiritual profit, and to push and strain them up to something to which they are not really called and of which they do not know what to make. That his conscience did not upbraid him in this matter for the many later years of his priestly and episcopal life; and that as to those first years he hoped that he had not been as unwise as he might have been.

Also, an experienced old priest (himself an early convert to the Roman Catholic Church) once told me that he had long found it a bad sign when *converts* were not at least inclined to be active proselytisers. That with *born* Roman Catholics it was different: these could be thoroughly zealous in their religion, and yet not be thus active, or inclined to be thus active.

As to myself, I find myself inclined to be very zealous to help souls to make the most of what they already have; and, if they come to think of moving, to test them to the uttermost. And again, to do all I can to make the old Church as inhabitable *intellectually* as ever I can—not because the intellect is the most important thing in religion—it is not; but because the old Church already possesses in full the knowledge and the aids to *spirituality*, whilst, for various reasons which would fill a volume, it is much less strong as regards the needs, rights and duties of the mental life. This my second zeal includes the ardent wish and hope of serving sore and sulky, fallen-off or falling-off Roman Catholics—to heal their wounds and bring them back. *One* fallen-away Roman Catholic gives me more pain than a *hundred* accessions to the Church give me joy: For it is the *sticking it* which really matters in these things and which is difficult.

As to Mother Julian, where on earth has my Gwen-child acquired the notion that she was an Anglican! An Anglican in A.D. 1360? My Gwen, we must do some Church history later on! Of course she accepted the Pope as she accepted Christ and as she accepted God; although there was then no occasion to put this forward.

What you say about prayer, Sweet, is all very true, very solid. I know well what you mean. But though we will

most rightly shrink from saying that this or that in it is
God: yet it is God, His Reality, His Distinctness from yet
great Closeness to us, it is this grand Over-againstness
which through, and in, and on occasion of what you de-
scribe we experience in our little degree. What comes last
in our analysis of such states, is first in real existence. I
enclose for you a little article which (as all except my big
book) was spontaneously asked of me, title included. Do
not, Dear, dwell much upon or worry about the Pope. It is
not for *that* that I send it to you. Nor do I want you to
lend it for that to others who might be pressed or worried
by it. I send it because of the *contrata* bit; and because I
am utterly sure that this is the direct antidote to the all
but universal Pantheism of our times. Before people worry
about the Church or even about Christ, they must be
helped to get God—their notions as to God—sound and
strong.

I also include a fine letter of Mrs. Clement Webb, because you will admire what she says about suffering, and
because of the charming bit about Richard and yourself. I
do not require it back.

As to the Sadhu, I feel with you that we ought never to
forget his non-Europeanness. How strange that *profound*
difference between East and West. Why, in some real way,
the Sadhu, all Christian though he be, is further away than
are Plato and even Socrates! The Sadhu's visions are
strangely wooden, *leathery* things, astonishingly other
than, and inferior to, the revelations or visions of Mother
Julian or of St. Teresa. It is in this matter especially that
the object of the book—its object in the mind of Streeter,
not, I think of Appasamy—is not attained: the object being to show that a man as entirely outside of any Christian body or Church, can be as deep and delicate, as valuable a mystic, as are the mystics belonging to the Church.
Streeter really proves the opposite of what he wants to
prove.

## Baron Friedrich von Hügel

As to Plato, I am delighted you are taking to him so strongly. I hope you will end by being steeped in him by having read all the Dialogues we have fixed upon at least four times each; and that you will come to be able to compare Dialogue with Dialogue, and to use Plato generally, for comparison and criticism in your non-Platonic reading. I am trying to follow you in these your Plato readings: have so done the *Protagoras* and half of the *Gorgias*. So glad you are at the *Phædrus* and soon at the *Symposium*. And mind to admire the *Meno* — I love it!

As to taking the three children abroad for those three months, how excellent! Yet there is one modification of your plan which (but for possible valid reasons contrary, unknown to me) would seem an improvement to me. You very rightly regret the lack of German and Italian among you four. But why not hold out Germany and Italy as a reward, some other year, of German and Italian acquired at least by *some* of you? You would this coming 1922 go to *France* and, if you liked, *French* Switzerland, staying, say, a week or ten days in Paris — there seeing thoroughly the great galleries, Versailles, Fontainebleau, etc. Then to the great cathedral cities — Rouen, Tours, Orleans, etc., and staying quietly, for, say, a month, in Brittany, there really to know that fine earnest race. I am very sure that staying in new countries, amongst other races, is an immensely educative influence. But you must really stay with them, speaking their language, sharing their life. And I am equally sure that mere *travel*, mere maximum moving about, is sterilising rather than improving.

Loving old Uncle-Father,

H.

*Letters to a Niece*

13 VICARAGE GATE, W 8

*13 December 1921*

So glad you have got the books, and letters—and article packet. No hurry for a letter from you, though it will be most welcome when it comes!

This is merely to express my distress that you should have attempted Plato's *Parmenides* or the *Philebus*. Have you forgotten how we settled that you would not touch any of the six Critical Dialogues, as all being far too difficult? I think that resolution most important, as otherwise you will get bewildered, strained, and then sick of Plato. You have plenty of him to read: *Meno, Cratylus*, the *Republic*—as long as four or five ordinary Dialogues—and the *Laws*, even longer; and then all over again and again, comparing one with the others.

As to the Curé d'Ars pray read the two big volumes before the little one. You will see how sweet old Mlle. Ars is also.

F.v.H.

13 VICARAGE GATE, LONDON, W. 8

*20 January 1922*

Here I am, my darling Gwen-Child, scribbling to you after getting released, only last night at eleven-thirty (when I could turn into bed), from my last three weeks' grind. I wonder a little, sometimes, my little old thing, whether you quite realise the costingness of my life—what a lot it necessarily takes out of me, how little of nerve and brain force it leaves me, when my direct work of thinking and exploring in and with Faith, Love and Practice has been done? You see I cannot apprehend anything seriously without tension, I mean my very way of taking anything involves much tension. And this is why there readily come misgivings to me when I gain any great influence either with young men or with women (whether young or not). For both these sets of God's creatures—of my fellow-creatures—cannot, I think, stand much tension. They either break down physically under it, or their faith collapses under the strain, or (the best that can happen to them) they either get away from such strongly *tensional* individuals, or learn to dwell in such individuals, upon the harmonies in them and not the tensions—anyhow, my Dearie, the costliness, at least to myself, of the kind of work I have again been at, *plus* the *endless* business, friendliness, etc., of the time of year, have alone caused my silence.

I find that I have four letters from you unanswered, except by a post card for the first, and another post card for the last one. I will first write some words about each of your chief points and, indeed, about yourself generally. And I will then tell the chief doings and experiencings since last I wrote you a letter.

First as to the letter 13 December. I am so glad that you then, and later on again, liked the Curé d'Ars so much. It seems to me you could, with great profit, absorb into your life pretty well the whole of him—in his darling simplicity, his continuous self-oblivion, his absorption in God, and yet his amazingly large attention to others, especially to the poor and the lost. I have just now been again using him amongst my illustrations, and as always, with the greatest confidence and consolation. You know that at Thekla's convent the very experienced prioress has placed a statuette (a beautiful one) of the curé in prayer on to the table in the centre of their chapter house, as an encouragement to them to persevere in their—in his—in their joint kind of prayer of pure love.

Then I am so glad you love Plato's *Meno* so; it is one of my favourite dialogues—perhaps the one which I carry most constantly in my head.

Then there is the strange but very dear old clergyman (here are his, somehow very sweet, letters back, with thanks). I am very glad he has got you to read Scott's *Heart of Midlothian*—a book I know well and admire much. I am a bit surprised you had never read it. But have you already noted one thing, Sweet? That dear old cleric—I feel quite sure—is one more living refutation of the "all men have something to hide" doctrine. There is *that* about him which cannot coexist with any sex impurity. Either he has never lost his baptismal innocence (the more likely alternative I think), or he has long and long ago fully, deeply repented of any early lapses that may have occurred. St. Augustine is there to prove to all men of good faith that such recovery is fully possible.

In this same letter you dwell upon how one helpful spiritual writer after the other turns out to be Roman Catholic, whereas the Protestant bodies, even Anglicanism, have, most at least, to go to those others for spiritual classics. I think this is no prejudice of yours, my Gwen-child. But I think a *certain* advantage is extant on the other side. Not, I think, in Protestantism *as such* even there; but because, alongside of much licence, Protestantism has at least ended by leaving liberty to scholars. I mean even such liberty as is necessary for a really cogent defence of the Catholic Faith. The official representatives of the Catholic Church, on the contrary, have mostly, or generally, struck away from such liberty. Yet this advantage of Protestantism is immediately lost by it when it becomes pointedly, polemically Protestant; it is then at once more narrow and unseeing than is the narrowest Roman Catholicism. And certainly the finest Roman Catholic scholars, when and where they are allowed elbow-room, remain the worthy descendants of those Roman Catholic scholars who—so Mabillon the Benedictine, Richard Simon the Oratorian, and Denys Petau the Jesuit, all in the seventeenth century—were respectively the founders of the science of history, of Biblical criticism, and of the history of Christian dogma.

As to the letter of 21 December. You understand, of course, that I have excluded that group of Plato's Dialogues from your reading, only because of their great technicality and difficulty. If the day comes when, having read and re-read all the others, you feel you know them so well that you could understand fresh problems raised by him upon the conclusions reached by him so far, you could *then* try your hand at these dialogues also. Fortunately these dialogues are much the least beautiful in form, and contain least of sayings directly utilisable for religion or ethics. But they are free from any such blemishes as appear in the *Symposium* and the *Republic*.

I shall love your getting back to Plato.

Perhaps, by now, you have seen that review of my book in the *Times Literary Supplement*, and my letter there in answer to it. Mr. Bruce Richmond has written me the kindest letter about it all—that he had wished to give me pleasure, and was so sorry he had failed. But he added what took all distress about the incident out of my mind—that the review was not, as I thought, by Canon Barnes (one of the canons of Westminster Abbey), who, in a review of a book by Dean Inge, had written a *most* handsome sentence about my writings, and who (I sadly thought) had now changed his mind about my work. I still believe that my letter was more or less necessary; but I see, as a friend points out, that I have missed one of the chief difficulties in cases such as that of Anthony Trollope—that he, Anthony Trollope, was, highly probably, baptised, and validly baptised. Yet baptism, according to the universal orthodox doctrine, implants in the baptised soul the seeds of the supernatural life.

If I wrote the letter now, I would still bring up the Anthony Trollopes of the world, but would declare that I had never yet found a fully satisfactory answer to the problem presented by such baptised persons, even though I continued to feel that a doctrine, equivalent to the ancient doctrine of *Limbo*, could be fruitfully used in face of the problem of the apparently purely *natural* goodness of at least many of the unbaptised.

And then the pathetic bit about your gardener's father so ill; and the gardener's wife your only usual companion at Holy Communion!

Then your letter of 29 December showed so well how much and how exactly rightly you feel about Christmas — that immensely warm and expansive, lowly and homely, utterly touching feast. And I love to think of David at Holy Communion with you there, and then you and Olivia at a service in the cathedral. — And then came the funeral of your gardener's father.

What you say of the ignorance of the poor about Our Lord and their practical heathenism is sad indeed, yet I believe it true.

As to the young convert living out in the fields, I too wonder about him. I mean, that he is being straight and devoted is plain enough. But is he being wise? And has he anyone wise to advise him, and does he attend to such an one?

First, off and on during December I had a good deal to do to help a lady whom I have known for, I think, fifteen years at least, a woman who has much religious influence with many souls; and who, if she succeeds in becoming more harmonious and more deep in herself, will do much pure good instead of as now, I think, not a little harm mixed with some good. She asked me to help her in all her spiritual views, practices, etc. First she wrote me out — very humbly and simply — as to where she stood, etc. I drew up, in response, a rough set of rules and proposals which she came here for me to develop to her. She was then asked to let me have a second report as to how the proposals struck her for direct execution in her life. And

the second report she then furnished was carefully criti-
cised by me in my final advice to her, which grew into a
bulky affair. It was impossible to be much shorter with a
person who has read very much and thought very much;
who began as a Pantheistically-inclined Agnostic; and
who, although she now, I am happy to say, goes to Anglican Holy Communion, and indeed also to Mass, and even
to Benediction at the Carmelites here, never, I found,
prays to Our Lord; indeed she declared that she never
could do so! — She has undertaken to carry out, in great
simplicity, the proposals which I ended by making very
definite. She would strive gently to bring consistency into
her life, by at least *thinking of* Our Lord at Holy Communion; and she would give as much time to visiting, and
to attending to, the poor, as ever she could without ne-
glecting other duties. She has settled now to give two afternoons a week to them; and to try and learn by their
needs — the need of religion of a definitely historical kind —
the need of Our Lord, His Life, His Death, His Sacred Person. She is to report at midsummer how things have gone.
My Gwen; you who have the great grace to love and to
worship Christ our Lord, pray for this soul, please. I
promise to tell you how she gets on. But, purposely, I am
not going to see her in between-whiles.

Then I have had vividly brought home to me a difficulty (a purely social, educational difficulty which all my
life has dogged my steps) — as to what degree of experience, learning, tension, etc., is good and wise or such and
such for young people, or (even generally) for people generally. You see, I had felt so glad and proud at the
thought of Professor Troeltsch coming with me, next July,
to Swanwick, where he would address some seven hundred young men and young women university students
on religion. I felt so sure that the Christian Student
Movement authorities would accept this, that I told
Troeltsch of my efforts, adding that the thing could be

quite sure only after the Executive Committee had decided in September. But when, at end of November, I still had received no news, I wrote to the Secretary, Christian Student Movement, asking what had become of the plan, and Mr. Tatlow answered that as soon as he had put the plan to the Executive Committee (all university students), the large majority at once protested hotly against it. That the Christian Student Movement Statutes opened out with a declaration that only Christians who accept the historic Creeds could belong to the movement; that surely also only such Christians could be asked by the Committee to speak to the young people at this, their supremely *religious*, gathering; and that if once they let in Professor Troeltsch, they would not be able to exclude from their platforms Quakers or Unitarians or Theosophists. That my own case was distinctly different—that they would much like to have me; but, as to Troeltsch, no. Mr. Tatlow added that a small minority did want to have him; and that he had thought the matter so important, that he was asking a certain number of experienced mature friends of the movement what they would have him do. And that, meanwhile, he would like me to tell him clearly why I had thought of Troeltsch for them, and again how I felt, now that I had their statutes and this opposition so plainly before me. To this I answered that I had been close friends and the most careful student with and of Troeltsch for some thirty-five years; that, all that time, I had learnt nothing but good, and the rarest good, from him, since he had helped me greatly to keep and to increase a joyous faith in God, and had brought me back to a full (and fuller than ever) admiration of the Golden Middle Age. That a Quaker, several liberal Lutherans (like Troeltsch), and a Unitarian had much helped me religiously, I mean right up to the consolidation of my historic, Roman Catholic, Christian faith. Hence I had felt these young people might greatly profit, and would hardly suffer

damage from Troeltsch. — That the mere fact of their statutes did not arrest me, since even the best rules (and these
seemed very good) were liable to exceptions. And that I
continued to feel it very difficult to believe that even people so young as his [*sic*] should not be exposed to influence far more dangerous than could be the influence of
Troeltsch in his least orthodox strain. Besides, that
Troeltsch had spontaneously undertaken not to speak a
word which had not previously been considered by me.
And yet that his, Mr. Tatlow's, communication *had* pulled
me up in this wise, that I had been made to remember
that I was at least thirty-five when Troeltsch first came
into my life, and a fully formed man, whereas these young
people were all between eighteen and twenty-four. And
then I had had to recognise how; I had, more than once
(and once to a saddening degree), myself presupposed
too much maturity, too much carrying power in those I
had influenced, and this had had, for long, very sad results. So that, unless the seniors he had referred the matter
to were practically all for Troeltsch, I wanted him, Mr.
Tatlow to decide against asking him to Swanwick. End of
December, Mr. Tatlow wrote, definitely declining to have
Professor Troeltsch at Swanwick; that I still did not realise
what immature, unformed, callow, ignorant minds they
had to deal with. But that the officials — the mature and
paid men — of the movement would esteem it an honour
to listen to Troeltsch next September, at their London
meeting. I have still to write to Troeltsch that the Swanwick thing is off, and that I do not think the London thing
would be worth his coming all that way. I shrink from
doing so, as it may a bit pain that very sensitive man; but
I must just do it, as well as I can!

And then, lastly, these last three weeks have been chock
full of "Priest and Prophet."

I ended by scribbling out in pencil a MS. so long that,
though I spoke for seventy minutes, I could only use up a

little over a third of the whole. I learnt a lot in working it out. I think the chief points which I got to see more clearly than ever before were that Jesus was in conflict, roughly speaking, not with the priests — *that* came only quite at the end, but with the Pharisees, who were all *laymen to a man*; and again that the reason of Our Lord's vehemence against them was because, claiming to be the religious teachers of the people at large, they made religion unbearably heavy and complicated for *the poor* — the poor being precisely those to whom He had come to preach the Good Tidings. This preaching to the poor, He had placed as the culminating work and credential of His life, in His great answer to the inquiry of John the Baptist; and hence the glorious "Come unto Me," and the "laden and heavy burdened," with *His* contrasting "yoke" which is "sweet," and *His* burden which is light, aims, in the first instance, at the Pharisees. Now the descendants of the Pharisees are, quite plainly, not (at least not necessarily) priests, but such over-cultivated Puritan lay theologians as, e.g. the Unitarians. They, too, have no Gospel for the poor, whereas Jesus has, and first of all for *them*; you and I come afterwards! — Also, the priests still, in Jesus's time, stood for friendly contacts with matter; the Pharisees, for vigilant hostility to all such contacts. True, the Pharisees practised endless washings; but these were for purification from all sorts of contacts: with matter of all kinds. And true, also, the priests practised ablutions; yes, but they practised them as preparations for contact with other kinds of matter, in the sacrifice, the anointings, incense, etc. Jesus stands out quite plainly on the contacts side: so in the Curé of the woman with the issue of blood, of the lepers, etc. All these things were an abomination to the Pharisees.

Well now, Sweet, good night! Oh, may you succeed in not over-straining your precious health and in managing some grand rest, expansion and peace.

God bless you. Pray for me.
Loving old,
Uncle-Father.

13 VICARAGE GATE, LONDON, W. 8

*24 January 1922*

Darling Child,
This only in answer to the confession questions.

1. You have hit upon the very difficulty which I fore-
saw for you in any at all frequent confession. It is one
which you would feel, far more definitely, if you were a
Roman Catholic, having to confess (if a frequent commu-
nicant) at least every three weeks, as I do.

2. Confession is for sins, and nothing else. Hence no
confession of general unworthiness, also no confession of
general imperfections of your natural character – that you
are too sensitive, too vehement, etc.: all quite true, but no
more for confession than that your nose is too long. St.
François de Sales was a good while in getting St. Chantale
out of the way of confessing such constitutional defects.

3. Give yourself not more than fifteen minutes *at most*
of quiet, leisurely, circumspect, warm and loving preparation – gently recalling the situations in which you have
been since last confession: all this after, of course, asking
Our Lord to give you light and love for seeing. If anything
then pricks you – keep that for your confession, always
confessing first whatever may be most difficult to confess,
then make a gentle, quiet firm, but *not straining*, act of
contrition. And after all this *no deliberate recurrence to the
subject.*

4. If nothing thus pricks you – no strain, no trouble, no
occupation with this fact. But, if you do go to confession
notwithstanding, simply explain that you could find
nothing committed since the last confession, so and so
long ago; and re-confess the biggest thing you confessed

before—but very gently, with your soul turned to Christ, your light and love and life.

5. If Edward Talbot recommends you to go to confession thus often (every six months) I should like you to go, otherwise, to spread out the time even more. For, as you know, in the Church's early centuries, the faithful (saintly souls included) went only for grave sin, in public confession, to the bishop. We must not expect, I do not want *that* back. Still, the relation between more or less deliberate *sin* and confession it is certainly wise to keep up, as far as possible, and not to let one's confessions degenerate into a sort of flea-hunt, a straining to discover sins.

Pray for me.

Loving old Uncle,

F.v.H.

13 VICARAGE GATE, W. 8

*28 February 1922*

My darling Gwen-Child,

I *was* sorry to see your half-sheet to Aunt Mary this morning—I mean, as to your chill and sickness. For, as to your coming here for those nights, it is, of course, delicious. We *both* like this, very much. And we will have, I trust, at least two talks, won't we? I can easily manage such in the afternoons. Friday and Saturday, I have teaching; but even then we would arrange—or for after dinner—though, no, *that* is Aunt Mary's time with you.

Aunt Mary thinks you will have caught this chill in this my study, which is, of course, a further reason for distress. But I undertake to have a good fire alight half an hour before you turn up in here, unless the weather is truly summery. I trust, though, you will now be quickly right again. You said nothing about headaches; I trust that means they have hardly molested you lately. After our talk I had some scruples—I felt that I had, somehow, been straining your brain, and *that* for matters more of general *religiosity* than of the definite religion we love. I will try to do better next time. — Also I never asked after the children — their health; whilst you asked so nicely after us three. Well, I also write because I like to be in touch with you on starting Lent to-morrow. I am again cutting myself off from buying any books for myself till after Easter. But *that* would hardly do for you, you buy, doubtless, so few, Sweet. You have so many trials sent you by God, Dearie — your headaches, housework (when considerable), money anxieties and bigger trials still, that I suspect the trying to meet and utilise all this extra well during the forty days will be all, and quite enough, for you, unless Edward Talbot has made some suggestions — they would be sure to be wise. I have been having a strange correspondence with Loisy, on a point which shows how strangely unalive he is to the most obvious evidences counter to his utterly inadequate *Religion of Humanity.* He actually claims that M. Littré's last months — that all that M. Huvelin observed then — is a fine illustration of this, Loisy's, present conception of religion. Whereas, of course, it is precisely the opposite. M. Littré had lived fifty years a believer in, and propagator of, that "Religion." And then God sent him an experience which made him feel a new world in process of revealing itself to him, in which a keen sense of sin, a deep contrition, were central. Loisy argues that because M. Littré did not die an explicit Catholic or Christian, or even Theist, there was no change within the "Religion of Humanity." Strange obtuseness in one usually so even excessively awake! Well, Sweet, get well, Blessing; don't overwork either body or mind or soul. God loves you and touches you to love Him. What more do we want?

Loving old Fatherly,
F.v.H.

You must not hurry on the readings, all can wait! At Holy Communion for you to-morrow morning, Child.

13 VICARAGE GATE, W. 8

*11 April 1922*

My darling Gwen-Child,

I want you to get a letter from me on the day of Olivia's confirmation. Indeed I have also written herself a little one — enclosed — which pray give to her.

I so love to trust and believe that she will take the act really seriously, and that the Christian's fight against "self" — whatever may be the particular form and degree of "self" in the particular soul — will begin, or rather will grow deeper and firmer, with her to-morrow.

My darling Niece-Child! *How* happy I am to think of you in bed, and in bed, and in bed, and not doing *anything*, not even reading, beyond just what your strength permits! What a lot we can grow spiritually — that is, how much more solidly anchored in the peace and beatitude of God we can become — by simply thus resigning ourselves, as cheerfully as possible, to such do-nothing, which indeed, where and when nature requires it, can be most refreshing. I am so glad, too, you listen and watch the birds. I shall try and get for you a "remainder" copy (the book is quite out of print) of Alfred Newton's *Dictionary of Birds* — a truly engrossing work. There you can read up all about the particular habits, migrations, etc., of each of these birds.

I have striven to find for you those L.S.S.R. remarks of mine on the four papers about God — so far without success. But I do not doubt I shall end by finding and sending you them. The two Beaconsfield addresses are, I find, in a lady's hands, who has promised their early return. These also you shall have as soon as I get them back, but to-day I send you something that I spoke a week ago at an extra meeting of our L.S.S.R. The copy of my remarks is for you to keep; the abstract of Mr. Joseph Wicksteed's paper is for you to return some time, when quite done with. Joseph Wicksteed is the son of that very noble man—certainly a most striking intelligence—Philip Wicksteed (great on Dante and Aquinas).

I was very happy, though, whilst working at this criticism of mine; my toil at my new book helped me greatly there. I loved both your little letters, dear Child; but never write when feeling too tired—you shall have a copy, all your own, of Charles Foucauld; but just at this moment I have lent *this* copy, which I wanted to return to you at once, to a man friend. I felt that Foucauld's heroic life would draw him, somehow, out of his deep depression.

Have you thought of Scott's Waverley Novels for reading, when you want to read and yet are too tired for harder books? I think you do not know them—certainly not all; the *Heart of Midlothian* was new to you—you would find *The Antiquary, Old Mortality, Rob Roy, Quentin Durward, Kenilworth, Fortunes of Nigel, Peveril of the Peak*; first rate. But I will not press you, because I myself, when very tired, find but little help in novels; to lie in the dark room or to prowl in the open with Puck—that does me far more good!

We shall love to have you for that night; and if you could turn up by five or even six, you and I might have a good talk before dinner—I shall keep myself free for *that*; after dinner I shall want Aunt Mary to have you.—I will show you that big history of De Rancé and the beginnings of the Trappists, because I fancy it would much interest you; as sometimes a long detailed book is better for browsing through, when one is ill, than are shorter, more concentrated affairs. Darling Puck has a cyst on the right side of his neck—was with the vet. yesterday—but this very experienced man says that we can enjoy the darling little friend still for several years. How stupid of me to think you could walk about and stand, etc., amongst your poor! But London shopping—that, too, is surely not the thing for you! Limit it and the like, Dear, all you can, pray!

Loving old Uncle,

F.v.H.

On Maundy Thursday, day after to-morrow, at my Holy Communion, on that, one of my dearest days, the little old Niece-Child will, of course, be very specially prayed for, and Olivia, indeed all three, and H—too! God bless you, Child.

13 VICARAGE GATE, KENSINGTON

*From letter of 23 May 1922*

I am most glad you specially love the Psalms for vocal prayer—you are here, as I find so generally with you, entirely in the mind of the Church. But I trust that you do not neglect the Our Father, the Apostles' Creed, and the Acts of Faith, Hope and Charity and Contrition—the first and these last in all your morning and night prayers.—My business began with that meeting of our L.S.S.R. in this house, when I tried to show that Our Lord's vehemence against the Pharisees was indeed sincere, and must be taken by us as indicating grave error in the Pharisees, yet that it also was a revival, after some six hundred years, of the old, pre-exilic tone and form of prophetic denunciation. Amos, Hosea, Isaiah, Jeremiah, they all, pretty well unbrokenly, speak as though the only sinners on the land were the men who went to church!—as though only a quite perfect moral life (an ideal never quite attained) left public worship anything but a thing without value to God or man—indeed a thing abominable to God and His prophets. There is quite demonstrably here a certain exaggeration, an "either ... or," instead of "both ... and." History teaches us quite plainly that there exists no such thing as strong and persistent religion without public worship, and no public worship which supports itself under and by pure contemptuous toleration or cheery matter-of-courseness. Public worship requires much care, much nurture: does it deserve all these pains? Why, of course, *yes*, and *Yes* again.

Then my dear friend Duchesne's death, on 21 April, but known to me only on 30 April, gave me from 3 May to 17 May much, much trouble and some anxiety in the study of his letters to me and the making up of my mind what to insert in my letter to the T.L.S., and how much to tell of the difficult matters of debate which so largely filled his life and my feelings and judgments. The thing was to have appeared this week, but is now put off to next week—a truly difficult thing. But, mind, Dear, he was not "père"—not a religious, but simply a secular priest, like Abbé Huvelin. Then came the final settlements with Mr. Thorold for his seeing my *Mystical Element* through the press.

Then, on 17 May, tea with a sweet old, one-legged, Jewish gentleman, full of woe as to the rampant anti-Semitism of our day. A dear old thing; must talk about him another time.

And then, 10-20 May, to Cambridge, with Aunt Mary, for my brother's honorary degree and garden-party. Hillie came down for the day. My little old thing: this really must do for now. God bless you, and make you well, and help you to live, for these months, as much just simply for getting well as ever you can. I trust once at Peg Antrim's you will be in clover for these purposes. Drop, then, all else.

Loving old Uncle-Father,

F. v. H.

I send you nothing till you ask, indeed that is not important, nothing is, except what may help you to rest and to get well.

13 VICARAGE GATE

*29 June 1922*

My darling Gwen-Child,

This is the day of my first Holy Communion fifty-five years ago! So I *must* just write you a scrap at last! For *that* should be the very centre of a Christian's devotional life; to live up to *that*, no one can; but Christ can and will help, if only we are attentive and generous. I really could not write these last—nearly three weeks, I fear it is. For I began with a very distinct nervous breakdown—such an old acquaintance that! Why, from eighteen to nearly thirty my life was pretty well blotted out by such troubles! They are very salutary for one, I find—they make one feel one's utter dependence upon God, even for getting away from utter self-absorption, which then seizes one all round. Nothing but dark rooms and much open air then possible, but *that* is infallible as a gradual restorative—after a week or ten days.

Since then I have been in a condition of brainwork in the night, when deep points where I have been struck for the last two years are getting wonderfully clear. But this also is very wearing, and also humbles one finely. I no more know how these lights are reached than I know how a penny in the slot should issue in a good, right railway ticket. Two nights ago I had such absorbing pains of a kind I knew well—those which began the months of trouble which ended, twice, in big operations, that went round yesterday to the surgeon that did them. But he found, for quite certain, that nothing of the kind was preparing, and that all the parts concerned are in perfect condition. That the pain was sciatica or rheumatism seizing hold of the old parts, because specially sensitive, I suppose, after all those happenings; this was a great relief to know, for otherwise my Giffords would have become uncertain.

Now, as to yourself, Child. I quite see the reason for your settling in London—it seems to me unanswerable, and that neither your love of the country nor H——'s dislike of such a move should deter you from it. After all, by getting high up and with some open space and greenery around you, it need not be emphatically towny. I at once inquired of Mrs. Stuart-Moore, whom [you] now know well, and who has lived for years on the highest part here, in Campden Hill Square. Please, Dear, note carefully what she writes in the two notes enclosed. The second note is entirely about this matter. Pray specially note *what I have underlined in blue*, in the first note. You will see what a warm, kind soul she is! Don't want these back, second half of first note was too private to send on.

Hope to write about emotion soon.

How excellent Lundy island sounds!

Loving,

Uncle-Father.

THURSLEY, NEAR GODALMING, SURREY

*21 August 1922*

My ever darling Gwen-Child,

What a wonderful place you have struck, for genuineness and always vital action and conviction! And yet there is also a further fact, to be deeply grateful for, that not only you yourself, but the three children too, possess tastes so direct and so genuine—so unspoilt by the "fine" world and by "good" society as to respond to it all and deeply to love it! Perhaps especially the letter of 18 August, received this morning, makes me feel this double gratitude for you, all four, very much indeed. Certainly, if such a place cannot keep people genuine, no place could! —You will be able to come back to it all every year, or at least often. But to live there entirely would hardly do, for any one of you four!

*Letters to a Niece*

I am struck with what you say about church—of people, even there, not going into it to pray out of service times. My difficulty about this springs from the fact that with us Roman Catholics the frequentation of our churches at such times springs, I think, entirely or all but entirely, from the Reserved Holy Eucharist, and our Devotion to It. I doubt whether *we* have got any more, or any very different, feeling, towards any church or chapel of our own where (a rare thing) there is no Reservation, than Protestants have towards their churches out of service-times. Now, though the Reservation of the Holy Eucharist is very old—we can trace it back well into pre-Constantinian times—yet the *Devotion* to the Reserved Holy Eucharist is not older in England than about A.D. 1330, and, I think, nowhere older than this anywhere. This is curious, because the Reservation was always reverent, and I know of no documents or facts to indicate that the Catholics of all those centuries disbelieved in the real Presence of Our Lord at such times—(the restriction of His Presence to the time between the consecration and the communion is, I believe, a purely Protestant notion). The Greek Russian Church, e.g., does not have it, but believes (and practises, or rather has no active devotion) exactly as Western Christendom believed and practised up to A.D. 1330 or so. What happened to and in the Catholic churches up to about 1330? outside of service-times, I mean. I *think* there must have been some praying there in between-whiles; yet I doubt whether there was as much as since the awakening of the Devotion to the Reserved Holy Eucharist. It is this Devotion and Confessions of Devotion which have largely built up the Roman Catholic saints these last six centuries. Whereas devotion to the Holy Eucharist at Mass and Communion only, and confessions of obligation, which built up the Roman Catholic saints in the first thirteen centuries.

## Baron Friedrich von Hügel

Am so glad to think you are coming to Vicarage Gate in September. I am to be in Thursley myself (the address on this letter will alone be wanted) till 7 September for certain; but I am keeping myself open to stay on till 14 September or even 21 September (*at most*), in case health still requires it. Yet of course I much want to see you at home. Aunt Mary will certainly like to see you — to have you stay — the longer, the better.

Loving Uncle-Father,
F.v.H.

*Three sets of books, October 1922.*

Two sets are for close study; the third set, a single book, is for lighter reading. Any one set can be studied, and the lighter book be read, at different times of the same day. But only one of the harder sets to be studied at the same time, and to be finished, before the second set is tackled.

1. *Three books (four volumes) on and of Aquinas.*

I. Philip Wicksteed on *The Reactions of St. Thomas Aquinas.*

A fine book by a lover of Aquinas. But Wicksteed is a Unitarian, and hence unperceptive as to *revealed* theology. Pray read twice, all the English parts (that is, only the lectures and *not* the *notes),* also the Preface (pages vii-xvi).

I would either omit Lecture III (pages 157-196) and the second half of Lecture IV (pages 260-78); or I would read it with aloofness and critical awakeness.

2. St. Thomas, *God and His Creatures.*

I would study all carefully, at least once. Pages 196-235 I would read and re-read, and copy out bits; glorious!

3. Aquinas *Ethicus,* two volumes.

I would read all at least once; and would carefully re-read and browse amongst the parts which specially help

*Letters to a Niece*

you. Be patient with your not understanding of much at
first.

13 VICARAGE GATE, W. 8

*26 May 1923*

My darling Gwen-Child,
Many thanks for prompt loan of this. Have taken all
the particulars I wanted now; so here it is back.

There is one thing I much want you to undertake, and
so to quiet me. *Promise you will instantly drop* EVERY WORD
OF DANTE'S INFERNO. I myself have never dared read more
than scraps of it. Go to the *Paradiso,* and study this again
and again. At first, each canto at least three times.

It would grieve me so if you get repelled by Dante, who
otherwise could — and *will* — become part of your food and
air — your daily food, your daily air.

I pray daily *specially* for what you told me of. God bless
and brace and bear with us all!

Loving old Fatherly Uncle,
F.v.H.

Am mending; but still, bedroom for two or three more
days.

13 VICARAGE GATE, KENSINGTON, W. 8

*11 July 1923*

My darling Gwen-Child,
A matter goes revolving in my head about you, which,
I think, I had better mention now, since you may be acting
on it before we meet again next Monday. You told me you
had promised — I did not catch whom — to read again — 's
last book; and indeed you took away my copy for the
purpose. I have been feeling somewhat cross with any-
body who would ask such a thing of you, since it doubtless means a wish that you may, after all, come to like the

164

*Baron Friedrich von Hügel*

book, and you may then praise it, to the pleasure of all the author's family. And I think you could get yourself to do so, or at least to try. I care much for that family and wish them every consolation, yet I cannot doubt that we none of us ought—that we none of us have the right—to put this kind of pressure upon others. And to enter into such an affectionate little plot is, surely, not good for one's straightness—for that complete sincerity which alone gives value and the power to produce genuine pleasure to our literary judgments. But this point, too—I mean the moral point here involved—is for you to decide upon and follow, not for me to impose upon you. I only bring it up because you might acquire the habit before you had fully made up your mind. And so that is *that!* It is simply for yourself, Child. Perfect simplicity, never forcing the note: this we will try and combine with kindliest reserve and softening judgments where we can. But *not* more. No court paid to families, etc.

Old Father,
F.v.H.

13 VICARAGE GATE, LONDON, W. 8

*22 October 1923*

My darling Child,

I loved getting your post card this morning—some two hours ago—and hearing you had had so beautiful a Retreat. Of course I am keenly looking forward to seeing you when you are back, and when we can hit off a day and time to fit us both—perhaps next Monday, as before. But I write because I want, if I can, promptly to get quite clear in my old mind a matter that has been a bit perplexing me. I have to take gas and have one molar out this afternoon; and gas again and another molar out some few days hence; and it will be joy indeed, if I find that I was simply mistaken in the following matter and learn this in

165

between the two little woes. You see, my Sweet, you used to write to me often—the oftener the better for me (provided the writing came spontaneously to you, *without a touch of obligation about it*). And I loved getting these letters and learnt not a little from them, even though, latterly, I was mostly too tired to answer by letter. And then you came to Thursley, and I loved our time—I felt we had no straining, etc., between us. You went off: well, and thenceforward, somehow, the letters ceased. A pencil note, merely as to health; then, quite shortly ago, a joint little letter to Aunt Mary and me—this was all during nine or ten weeks. But yesterday Hillie came and, among other things about other people, told me you had found me very tired at Thursley, and had felt you ought not, then, to put any questions to me. So I have come to think that probably you kept silent, also as to letters, for my sake— to save me even the reading of them.

This morning's post card is so entirely the darling daughter, that I feel Hillie's report must be covering all. And so I feel I had better at once explain that *if you have not written as formerly* (I mean as to the quantity) *on my account*, I trust you will promptly drop any such notion and practice. Your letters simply rest and refresh me. But this, because they feel quite unforced, because I feel you to write them simply as the bird sings. And so, *if you have kept yourself from writing, even partly, because of yourself—* because it strained or hipped or otherwise tried you—*do not write as formerly till this feeling, if God wills, disappears.* It has been the fear that, by telling you all this, I might put pressure upon you, Child, that has kept me so long from saying anything. But when this Retreat of yours came and went without any account of it, I felt I must, somehow, find out. You are, Sweet, a humble soul, and may have thought I attached no importance to your letters. *If it was all for my sake,* you might now write me an account of the Retreat, still all fresh in your memory.

*Baron Friedrich von Hügel*

Ever loving Uncle-Father,
H.

13 VICARAGE GATE

*All Saints' Eve, 1923*

My darling Child,
Here, for All Saints', is, at last, Elisabeth Leseur's *Journal* for you. Tried to get it ready-bound for you—but is not to be had like that; and I did not want to wait till I had got it bound for you—nowadays a long process. I have got, at same time, a copy of my own—so we can refer each other to anything we come upon we like very much. The three little books are simply the remaining volumes of the Temple Dante, not yet taken home by you. Mind you sometime read the *Monarchy* in the Latin Works volume. I loved getting your last *Zoo* and *National Gallery* letter. We must talk about all in it on Monday next. Have, at last, plunged again into my big book composition, which I find turns into a prayer and makes me very happy—was missing it greatly. But this will make all mornings impossible to me for anyone—even the child I am scribbling this to. May we have a very, very deep and dear All Saints'—the day of all the saints in all times and places and disguises—so much the most of them known to God alone; indeed the day also of the saintly bits, the saintly moments, etc., the beginnings of sanctity in souls, not otherwise saints at all, God be with us.
    Your loving,
    Father.

13 VICARAGE GATE, W. 8

*4 November 1923*

My darling Child,

Grateful thanks again, for the last interesting letters. I could not answer your practical question — as to the two hours taken by you in that church, at once; and even now I can write only by doing so when I ought not to do so — on Sunday, which works the full restfulness for me only if I do not break in upon it at all.

I think your decision wise as far as its *interior* goes — that it will not strain you, accustomed and so happy as you are to and in long prayer. But is it wise *with your health* to tie yourself down thus to fixed days and hours? I wonder. 'Tis for you to watch how the arrangement works; and if the health really and clearly interferes with it, to give it up, I think.

As to to-morrow, Child, I shall love to see you, as always, and shall be sorry if you do not come, as always. But I feel as though it would be right for me not to accept your not coming *your cold is still at a very fountainous stage*, since I am specially hopeful just now of avoiding grave, deep colds which would interfere with my resumed composition work — even perhaps my getting to our opening meeting of the L.S.S.R. at Mr. Montefiore's on Tuesday — day after to-morrow. But I trust your cold is getting fairly a *dry* one now, in which case, pray, pray, come, Sweet. In any case, mind to understand that the cold, in an acute condition, is the sole and complete objection to your coming.

I shall, otherwise, so greatly delight — over our hour after lunch here to-morrow.

I think Aunt Mary expects you fixedly already; if so, please telephone only if you are *not* coming.

Loving old Father-Uncle,

H.

*Baron Friedrich von Hügel*

Walter Frere, Bishop of Truro! Well, I hope and believe he will make a very good, because a supernaturally-minded, one.

How grand Elisabeth Leseur is — is she not?

H.

*17 March 1924*

Darling Child,

This is to dwell for a moment with you — in gratitude and deepest life-wishes for Olivia — seventeen to-day! Dear me! Clearly no more a child and yet, please God, with something of the child in her to the end! She is evidently an honourable, straight character, and God's grace and her own freely docile co-operation will slowly build up of all for something deep and tender. And this wants, too, for a moment, to dwell upon your renouncing this Retreat. I wish now I had said nothing whatever in criticism of your going thus a third-time a year to a Retreat. For it is difficult to see what precise harm there would be even in four such, provided they really brace and soothe you, the fact being that they are far more just times of escape from racket and to more prayer than usual. And again, I did and do see that having you at this Retreat would especially please Mrs. — —; and this too would be a pleasure surely not wrong, this although certainly such things ought primarily to be done because we ourselves require them. I do not propose your, after all, going, because to wobble up and down is never a good thing in itself; but if you have still left it half open and you still, at bottom, feel that *attrait* to it as just a (third) opportunity for more rest away, and prayer, then I incline not to abandon it, but quickly settle it up as a thing you are going to do.

169

I have written to Mrs. — — this morning, not about this, either way, but full of good will towards her, as indeed I ought to be.

Well, anyhow, to Thursday at one and two — much talk, Child.

Loving Fatherly One,
H.

13 VICARAGE GATE, KENSINGTON, W. 8

*12 August 1924*

My darling Gwen-Child, (Gertrude + 1915)

I have been rather pursued by the fear that you might not get your cheque in time for such cashing of it as you may care to effect before leaving London on Thursday; and so, although I am looking forward (and much) to seeing you to-morrow (Wednesday) I am sending it enclosed to-night so as to reach you at home to-morrow (Wednesday, first post). I suppose you reach Hanover Terrace to-night; and, in any case, this letter will await you safely in your house. If you do arrive to-night, you can (if you like) cash the cheque in the morning tomorrow. I also want to say that I have got St. Barnard's *Sermons on the Canticle of Canticles*, two volumes, for you. The volumes are stout but not large, so that I fancy you can easily take Volume I. to Lundy, if you like. It might be well to begin such a great new book out there. I was so glad all went so well at that interview you feared so much in anticipation. I was very pleased to get that letter, and now the little one. But how nice to be talking together tomorrow.

Hillie is still away for a little Surrey visit; and Aunt Mary *may* be still away to-morrow. My chair takes me out from three to five, and I have my tea at five. Juliet Mansell has to be at her rehearsals till about six-thirty. I should like you to arrive for your tea at five, and to come down

170

to me at five-thirty. Thus you will see Aunt Mary or Hillie, if either of them is back; and if you have to be alone—with Eva looking after you! It will be for only half an hour. Nothing in this letter wants an answer till you answer me by word of mouth as to the cheque and the book.

    Loving Fatherly Uncle,
    F.v.H.

13 VICARAGE GATE, KENSINGTON

*Sunday, 14 September 1924*

My darling Gwen-Child,
    I find Professor Kemp Smith is right, who scolded me for dictating him a long letter, for even that day it markedly diminished the benefit of my rest. But this is the last day of my holiday—I hope to begin work anew tomorrow, although this persistent wet throughout more or less all the six weeks has much limited the good derived from the rest. One long letter I could not help writing—to Sir Archibald Geikie, whose autobiography has been the great delight of my holiday, and who will be eighty-nine in December next—dear warm heart, and pure, still very (mentally) active and deeply religious life. As to a Jowett's *Plato* for Richard, I am carefully seeking a good, five-volume, copy—can well afford it for Christmas. When I have got it, I shall give it to you, for you to give to him. Say nothing of my intervention, please. I so love to think you say or imply literally *nothing* when (as so often) this is desirable. Hope Aunt Mary's letter has reached you; she told me she would write to you. Hillie has been staying with Beatrice Thynne.

    Loving Uncle,
    Freddy.

Printed in the United States
19978LVS00001B/499